Nutshells

Tort

in a Nutshell

AUSTRALIA AND NEW ZEALAND
The Law Book Company Ltd.
Sydney : Melbourne : Brisbane : Perth

CANADA
The Carswell Company Ltd.
Toronto : Calgary : Vancouver : Ottawa

INDIA
N. M. Tripathi Private Ltd.
Bombay
and
Eastern Law House Private Ltd.
Calcutta

M.P.P. House
Bangalore

ISRAEL
Steimatzky's Agency Ltd.
Jerusalem : Tel Aviv : Haifa

PAKISTAN
Pakistan Law House
Karachi

Nutshells

Tort

in a Nutshell

Ralph Tiernan, B.A.,
Senior Lecturer in Law,
Newcastle-upon-Tyne Polytechnic

London ● Sweet & Maxwell ● 1990

First Edition 1987
Reprinted 1987
Second Edition 1990

Published by Sweet and Maxwell Limited of
South Quay Plaza, 183 Marsh Wall, London E14 9FT
Laserset by P.B. Computer Typesetting,
Pickering, N. Yorks.
Printed by Richard Clay Ltd., Bungay, Suffolk

A CIP catalogue record
for this book is available
from the British Library.

Contents

CHAPTER 1

TRESPASS TO THE PERSON

Trespass to the person may take one of three forms, namely assault, battery or false imprisonment. The action of trespass will lie for any direct and immediate interference with personal liberty and is actionable without proof of damage. Although liability may at one time have been strict, it was held in *Stanley* v. *Powell* (H.C., 1891) that the defendant is not liable in the absence of negligence. As far as the burden of proof is concerned it used to be thought that the onus was on the defendant to prove affirmatively that he was not negligent. In *Fowler* v. *Lanning* (H.C., 1959), however, it was held that the burden in an action of unintentional trespass to the person was on the plaintiff to prove negligence. This was approved in *Letang* v. *Cooper* (C.A., 1965) in which Lord Denning M.R. went so far as to suggest that where injury is inflicted negligently, as opposed to intentionally, the proper cause of action is negligence and not trespass. Support for this view is to be found in *Wilson* v. *Pringle* (C.A., 1986).

BATTERY

A battery may be defined as the direct and intentional (or possibly negligent) application of physical force to the person of another without lawful justification. It is the act itself which must be intentional and there is certainly no requirement of an intention to cause injury. Whilst it would seem that any physical contact, however trivial, with another's person may constitute "force" for the purposes of the tort even though no bodily harm is done, the plaintiff must prove that the act was hostile. Thus, in *Cole* v. *Turner* (1704) it was said that the least touching of another in anger is a battery. According to *Wilson* v. *Pringle* (C.A., 1986) the existence or otherwise of hostility is a question of fact, but a hostile touching is not necessarily to be equated with ill-will or malevolence. In *Collins* v. *Wilcock* (H.C., 1984), for example, a police officer was held to have exceeded the scope of her duty by detaining a woman in circumstances falling short of an arrest, and therefore to have committed a battery. The court in *Pringle's* case had no doubt that, since the officer was acting contrary to the woman's legal right not to be physically restrained, the act of detention was hostile. As far as

the ordinary physical contacts of everyday life are concerned, such as
jostling in a crowded place or touching a person for the purpose of
engaging his attention, it is sometimes said that no battery is
committed because the plaintiff impliedly consents. In *Collins* v.
Wilcock the court said that cases of this nature should more properly
be treated as falling within a general exception embracing all physical
contact which is generally regarded as acceptable in the ordinary
conduct of daily life. An alternative way of approaching the matter
would be to say that there is no element of hostility in the
defendant's act.

Apart from the more obvious examples of striking another with a
fist or weapon, battery may take many forms. Thus, to spit in a man's
face or to throw water over him, or to seize something from his hand,
may be actionable wrongs, provided that the requirement of hostility
is satisfied. The defendant's act must be a positive one, voluntarily
done; merely to obstruct the plaintiff's passage by standing still is not
sufficient (*Innes* v. *Wylie* (1844)), just as there is no battery if the act
is done in a state of complete automatism. However, in *Fagan* v.
Metropolitan Police Commissioner (H.C., 1969) the defendant was
held liable for criminal assault in respect of what appeared, on the
face of it, to be a mere omission to act. The accused in that case
accidentally drove his car on to the foot of a police officer and then
deliberately delayed in removing the vehicle. One judge dissented on
the ground that at the time of driving onto the officer's foot the
defendant had no *mens rea*, and that after forming an intention to
allow the car to remain there he did no positive act. The reasoning of
the majority was that, where the defendant's act is a continuing one,
the *mens rea* need not be present at the inception of that act but
could, at some later time, be superimposed upon it.

One point which has still to be settled is whether the criminal law
doctrine of transferred intent applies equally to the civil law. The
problem arises where X, intending to strike Y, misses and hits Z by
mistake; in these circumstances X commits a criminal offence but it
remains undecided whether he would, in the absence of negligence,
be liable in tort.

As with all forms of trespass to the person the interference must be
direct in the sense that contact with the plaintiff must follow
immediately from the defendant's act. Thus, to place an obstruction
in the plaintiff's path with the intention that he should trip over it
may not be actionable as a trespass, though he may have a remedy
under the principle in *Wilkinson* v. *Downton* (H.C., 1897) (see later
in this chapter). On the other hand, to strike a horse whereby its
rider is thrown and injured has been held to constitute a battery

(*Dodwell* v. *Burford* (1670)). The difficulties inherent in determining whether the interference is sufficiently direct are well illustrated in *Scott* v. *Shepherd* (1773). The defendant threw a lighted squib into a crowded market-place, whereupon it was thrown by two others acting in defence of their person and property until it struck the plaintiff in the face and exploded, causing him the loss of an eye. The defendant was, by a majority, held liable in trespass, but one judge dissented on the ground that the action should properly have been brought in case because the injury was consequential rather than direct.

ASSAULT

An assault may be defined as an act which directly and intentionally (or possibly negligently) causes the plaintiff reasonably to apprehend that a battery is about to be inflicted upon him by the defendant. Although the term assault is popularly used to include a battery, a person may be guilty of an assault even though no battery is committed, for all that is required is the reasonable apprehension by the plaintiff of immediate violence. For example, to shake one's fist in another's face, or to aim a blow at him which is intercepted, is an assault, but the plaintiff must reasonably believe that the defendant has the means of carrying his threat into effect, so that there is no assault where the plaintiff is in such a position as to be inaccessible to physical force (*Stephens* v. *Myers* (1830)). Just as there may be an assault without a battery, so there may be a battery without assault, as where the plaintiff is struck from behind, or whilst asleep, by an unseen aggressor. Even if the defendant is for some reason unable to carry out his threat or equally has no intention of so doing, there seems to be no logical reason why he should not be guilty of an assault, provided that his act induces in the plaintiff a reasonable apprehension that force is about to be inflicted upon him. The most commonly cited illustration of this problem is that of pointing an unloaded gun at the plaintiff. In the civil case of *Blake* v. *Barnard* (1840) it appears to have been held that this would not constitute an assault, although one leading writer says that the decision may be explained on the ground that the plaintiff, having averred that a loaded gun was pointed at him, then sought a verdict on the basis that it was unloaded. In the criminal case of *R.* v. *St. George* (1840) the court was clearly of the view that it would be a common law assault to point an unloaded gun at the plaintiff (unless he knows it to be unloaded), and this would seem to be correct in principle.

As with battery there must be a positive act by the defendant, so that passive obstruction unaccompanied by any threatening move or gesture cannot amount to an assault (*Innes* v. *Wylie* (1844)). There is still doubt whether words alone may constitute an assault or whether some bodily movement is an essential requirement. In *Meade's Case* (1823) the view was expressed that "no words or singing are equivalent to an assault," but *dicta* in *R.* v. *Wilson* (H.C., 1955) point the opposite way. Whatever the position, words which accompany a threatening act may negative what would otherwise be an assault, as in *Tuberville* v. *Savage* (1669) where the defendant put his hand upon his sword and said: "If it were not assize-time, I would not take such language from you."

FALSE IMPRISONMENT

This may be defined as an act which directly and intentionally (or possibly negligently) places a total restraint upon the plaintiff's freedom of movement without lawful justification. The term "false" means wrongful and "imprisonment" signifies that the plaintiff has been deprived of his right to go where he will. Thus, a man may be imprisoned in his own home, in a motor car, or even in a public street, as long as his movements have been constrained by the defendant's will. Such constraint may be evidenced by the use of actual physical force amounting to an assault and battery, or simply by the reasonable apprehension of such force. But whilst the wrong of false imprisonment is often that of assault also, it is not necessarily so. For example, to lock a man in a room into which he has freely and voluntarily wandered is a false imprisonment but clearly not assault.

The act of imprisonment

It has been seen that there need be no imprisonment in the ordinary sense of the word. An unlawful arrest is in itself a false imprisonment, as is the continued detention of one who, though originally in lawful custody, has acquired a right to be discharged. The deprivation of the plaintiff's liberty must, however, be complete, and a mere partial interference with his freedom of movement is not an imprisonment. In *Bird* v. *Jones* (1845) the defendants wrongfully closed off part of a public footpath over Hammersmith Bridge. The plaintiff climbed into the enclosure but was refused permission to proceed and was told that he might make a detour by crossing to the other side of the bridge. There was held to be no false imprisonment. Provided the restraint is total, how large the area of confinement can be must depend on the circumstances of the case.

An imprisonment usually involves some positive act, and there is generally no duty to assist another to obtain his liberty. In *Herd* v. *Weardale Steel, Coke & Coal Co.* (H.L., 1915) the plaintiff miners wrongfully refused to do certain work in the mine and demanded that the defendants take them to the surface. The defendants refused for some 20 minutes to do so and, in an action for false imprisonment, it was held that the defendants' omission to accede to the plaintiffs' demands did not amount to an imprisonment. The plaintiffs had voluntarily accepted a restriction upon their liberty by initially going into the mine, and it was they who were in breach of contract by refusing to complete the shift. It may be that the defendants could have been liable had they been in breach of their own contractual duty. To similar effect is *Robinson* v. *Balmain New Ferry Co. Ltd.* (P.C., 1910) where the plaintiff, having paid a penny to enter the defendant's wharf to catch a ferry, discovered that he had just missed one and wished to leave. He was directed to the exit turnstile where he refused to pay a further penny which, as was clearly stated on a notice-board, was chargeable upon leaving. It was held that there was no false imprisonment because the plaintiff had entered the wharf upon the terms of a definite contract which involved him in leaving the premises by a different way upon payment of a small charge. These two cases could be regarded as supporting the view that a person who voluntarily accepts a contractual restraint upon his liberty cannot thereafter change his mind, in breach of contract, and demand that the restraint be terminated. This could be to take the matter too far, however, and it might be wondered what the position would have been if, for example, one of the miners in *Herd's* case had suffered an acute attack of claustrophobia.

The plaintiff's knowledge

A point of controversy is whether the plaintiff has a cause of action even though he is at the time unaware that he has been confined. In *Herring* v. *Boyle* (1834) it was held that the detention of a boy at school during the holidays for non-payment of fees by his parents was not actionable since the child was unaware of any restraint. Conversely, in *Meering* v. *Grahame-White Aviation Co. Ltd.* (C.A., 1919) the plaintiff voluntarily accompanied security police to a works office to answer questions about certain thefts from the company without realising that he was suspected. The police remained outside the office during the time that he was there, though the plaintiff was unaware of that fact. A majority of the court refused to disturb the jury's finding that the plaintiff had been unlawfully detained, though *Herring* v. *Boyle* does not seem to have been considered. In *Murray*

v. *Ministry of Defence* (H.L., 1988), however, a unanimous House of
Lords expressed a preference for *Meering* and took the view, *obiter*,
that knowledge on the plaintiff's part is not an essential ingredient of
the tort.

Means of escape

If a reasonable means of escape is available to the plaintiff there
may be no false imprisonment, for there cannot then be said to be a
total restraint. Whether the escape route is reasonable depends upon
the circumstances of the particular case, but it is unlikely to be
reasonable if the plaintiff is thereby exposed to the risk of injury to
his person or property. In *Wright* v. *Wilson* (1699) it was held not to
be false imprisonment where an escape could be effected by a
nominal trespass on the land of a third party. A hypothetical example
often given is that of the man who, whilst swimming naked, has his
clothes removed; in this case it is thought to be unreasonable to
expect him to expose his person in order to extricate himself from his
predicament. If the plaintiff does have the means of escape but is
unaware of it, the question is probably whether a reasonable man
would have realised that there was an available outlet. It is not
necessarily a defence that the plaintiff was not in fact being detained,
since the question again is what the reasonable man would have
thought.

Abuse of process

Wrongful arrest, for example by a police officer, is clearly a false
imprisonment, but no action of trespass will lie against one who has
procured the imprisonment of another by obtaining a court order,
even though that order may be erroneous. The appropriate remedy in
such a case is to sue for malicious prosecution or some other form of
abuse of legal procedure. The distinction lies in the fact that, in
making an order for the plaintiff's detention, a judicial officer does
not act as agent for the party who institutes the proceedings but
exercises his own independent judicial discretion.

INTENTIONAL PHYSICAL HARM

Where the defendant wilfully does an act, or makes a statement,
which is calculated to cause, and actually does cause, physical harm
to the plaintiff, he is liable in tort. This statement of principle was
laid down in *Wilkinson* v. *Downton* (H.C., 1897) where the
defendant was held liable for falsely telling the plaintiff, by way of a
perverted practical joke, that her husband had met with a serious

accident, in consequence of which she suffered physical illness through nervous shock. This case was approved in *Janvier* v. *Sweeney* (C.A., 1919) where, on similar facts, the defendant was again held liable for physical illness induced by shock.

It is generally thought that there is no reason for restricting this principle either to nervous shock or to statements. Thus, to poison a man's drink or to set traps for him upon one's land (as in *Bird* v. *Holbrook* (1828)), or to infect him with a disease, may be actionable under this principle. It is doubtful whether such acts are trespasses because they are not sufficiently direct.

A difficulty which arises is as to the meaning of "calculated to cause harm." If this simply means that the harm was such that a reasonable man would foresee it as a probable result, then there would appear to be an overlap with the tort of negligence. Perhaps a more likely interpretation of the phrase is that the harm must be of a kind that the defendant actually contemplated or intended to produce, bearing in mind that an intention can be imputed where what follows from the defendant's act is a natural and probable consequence of it.

DAMAGES IN TRESPASS

All forms of trespass are actionable *per se* without proof of damage, though nominal damages only may be awarded where no actual loss is suffered. Aggravated damages may be awarded where, for example, an assault or battery takes place in humiliating or undignified circumstances and, in an appropriate case, exemplary or punitive damages may be awarded.

DEFENCES

The following defences are available in an action of intentional trespass to the person:

Consent

If the plaintiff consents to an act which would, but for that consent, amount to the commission of a tort, the defendant has a good defence. Thus, the plaintiff may give his consent to physical contact within the rules of a lawful sport (*e.g.* a boxing match) or to the performance of a surgical operation. Even a consent to a criminal act may be a bar to subsequent civil proceedings (*Murphy* v. *Culhane* (C.A., 1977)), but a consent obtained by fraud or duress is invalid.

Contributory negligence

Although not free from doubt it appears that this may afford a defence (*Murphy* v. *Culhane* (C.A., 1977)).

Necessity

This may negative liability, provided that the occasion of necessity is not brought about by the defendant's own negligence. There can be very few instances, however, where it will apply to an intentional trespass to the person.

Defence of persons and property

A man may use such reasonable force as is necessary to protect either his own person or property, or that of another. What is reasonable is a question of fact depending upon the particular circumstances of the case. Reasonable force is similarly permissible to prevent the entry of, or to eject, a trespasser.

Reasonable chastisement

A parent may administer reasonable punishment to his child by way of correction. A schoolteacher may have a similar right, though the limits of this disciplinary power are uncertain in the light of changing public opinion on the issue.

Inevitable accident

Since the decision in *Fowler* v. *Lanning* (H.C., 1959) to the effect that the burden is upon the plaintiff to prove intention or negligence in an action for trespass to the person, it would appear that this is no longer a relevant defence.

Lawful authority

It is clearly a defence that the defendant was acting in support of the law. This is a particularly important defence in relation to powers of arrest and is beyond the scope of this book, falling more within the province of Constitutional Law.

CHAPTER 2

NEGLIGENCE: DUTY OF CARE

Negligence as a tort may be defined as the breach of a duty of care, owed by the defendant to the plaintiff, which results in damage to the plaintiff. The traditional division of negligence into its constituents of duty, breach and damage may be convenient for the purposes of exposition but tends to mask the fact that the issues involved frequently overlap.

THE NEIGHBOUR PRINCIPLE AND PROXIMITY

As the law developed it came to be recognised that certain relationships gave rise to a legal duty, such that carelessness by one of the parties in that relationship which caused damage to the other would entitle that other to bring an action for damages. In this way a number of specific "duty situations" was created, and a plaintiff who wished to sue had either to prove that his case fell within one of these existing categories of relationship or to persuade the court to recognise a new duty situation.

In *Donoghue* v. *Stevenson* (H.L., 1932) the plaintiff claimed to have suffered shock and gastroenteritis as a result of drinking a bottle of ginger beer which allegedly contained the remains of a decomposed snail. The drink had been bought for her by a friend from a cafe proprietor to whom the defendant manufacturers had sold it. The defendants argued that their duties in respect of products made by them were confined to the contract which they had with their buyers, but a majority of the House of Lords held that a manufacturer did, as a general rule, owe a duty of care to the ultimate consumer (see Chap. 6). A new duty situation was thus created but, more importantly, Lord Atkin purported to trace a common thread through existing authority and formulated a general principle—the "neighbour principle"—for determining whether, in any given case, a duty of care should exist. He said:

> "You must take reasonable care to avoid acts or omissions which you can reasonably foresee would be likely to injure your neighbour. Who then, in law, is my neighbour? The answer seems to be — persons who are so closely and directly affected by my act that I ought reasonably to have them in contemplation as being so affected when I am directing my mind to the acts or omissions which are called in question."

The significance of this principle was that it established negligence as an independent tort and provided a basis for its expansion to cover situations not governed by precedent, on the ground that damage was foreseeable. In *Home Office* v. *Dorset Yacht Co. Ltd.* (H.L., 1970) Lord Reid said that the time had come when the principle ought to apply unless there were some justification or valid explanation for its exclusion, a view subsequently endorsed in *Anns* v. *Merton London*

Borough Council (H.L., 1978) where Lord Wilberforce propounded a two-stage approach. In deciding whether a duty exists, he said, it is first necessary to see if there is a sufficient relationship of "proximity" between defendant and plaintiff, such that the former ought reasonably to contemplate that carelessness on his part may be likely to cause damage to the latter. If the answer to that be affirmative a prima facie duty of care arises. The court must then satisfy itself that there are no considerations "which ought to negative, or to reduce or limit the scope of the duty or the class of person to whom it is owed or the damages to which a breach of it may give rise."

The term "proximity" as used in the first stage of the test was regarded by many as synonymous with the neighbour principle and was therefore interpreted to mean that the criterion for establishing a prima facie duty was merely one of reasonable foresight of damage. Latterly, however, warnings have been sounded at the highest level against the danger of elevating the dictum of Lord Wilberforce to the status of a rule of law (*e.g. Governors of the Peabody Donation Fund* v. *Sir Lindsay Parkinson & Co. Ltd.* (H.L., 1985)), and in *Yuen Kun Yeu* v. *Attorney-General of Hong Kong* (P.C., 1987) Lord Keith said that the first limb of the test was not to be interpreted simply to mean that there would be a sufficient relationship of proximity whenever the defendant could reasonably contemplate likely harm. The expression "proximity or neighbourhood," he said, bore a wider meaning, importing the whole concept of necessary relationship between the parties, as envisaged by Lord Atkin when he spoke of neighbours as "persons who are so closely and directly affected by my act. . . ." His Lordship concluded that the term "proximity" was referable to ". . . such close and direct relations that the act complained of directly affects a person whom the person alleged to be bound to take care would know would be directly affected by his careless act." By thus investing "proximity" with a meaning going well beyond mere foreseeability, the prevailing trend has been to restrict the scope of negligence liability without the need for overt (or covert) consideration of policy factors (see below). In *Hill* v. *Chief Constable of West Yorkshire* (H.L., 1988) the plaintiff claimed in her capacity as administratrix of her daughter's estate, in respect of the murder of her daughter by a person whom, she alleged, the police had negligently failed to apprehend. It was held that, notwithstanding that harm to the daughter was reasonably foreseeable and regardless of policy considerations, there was insufficient proximity between the parties.

Thus far, it should be clear that reasonable foresight of likely harm is an essential, though not the sole, determinant of the existence of a duty. The concept of reasonable foreseeability is itself an extremely flexible one and can be readily manipulated to admit or deny recovery as the court perceives the justice of the case to demand. To say that a particular event was reasonably foreseeable may mean, at one end of the spectrum, that there was a very small chance of its happening, or, at the other end, that it was very likely to happen, and the language used by the judiciary serves only to show how broad and indeterminate the spectrum is. It is clear, however, that even where a particular type of damage is remediable in principle, the plaintiff will not be owed a duty if he was unforeseeable. For example, in *Bourhill* v. *Young* (H.L., 1943) a motorcyclist negligently collided with a tram and was killed. The plaintiff, who had just alighted from the tram, heard the sound of the crash, saw the aftermath of the accident some time later, and suffered nervous shock as a result. Her claim against the estate of the deceased motorcyclist failed on the ground that it was not reasonably foreseeable in the circumstances that she would suffer injury of any kind, physical or emotional. This is not to say that the plaintiff must be precisely identifiable; it is sufficient that he is a member of a class which the defendant ought to have had in his contemplation as foreseeably likely to be affected by his conduct (*Haley* v. *London Electricity Board* (H.L., 1965)).

A final point to note about "neighbourhood" and "proximity" is that these terms do not necessarily connote physical propinquity. Whether the parties are in close geographical proximity *may* be a relevant factor in determining the scope of the duty, if any (*e.g. Home Office* v. *Dorset Yacht Co. Ltd.* (H.L., 1970)). But there may be "legal" proximity without physical proximity (as, for example, between manufacturer and ultimate consumer), and vice versa (as, for example, where one trader causes financial loss to a rival by setting up in business next door).

PUBLIC POLICY

It has long been recognised that there are situations in which, as a matter of law, there is either no duty or a duty of limited scope only. In such cases, that damage to the plaintiff is foreseeable as a fact is irrelevant. In determining the issue of duty or no duty, factors to be weighed in the balance may be of a political, social or economic nature. Explicit reference to these so-called policy factors is to be found in the second stage of the *Anns* test, though there can be no doubt that the language of foreseeability and proximity is itself sufficiently flexible to admit of a consideration of the policy issues. In

Governors of the Peabody Donation Fund v. *Sir Lindsay Parkinson &
Co. Ltd.* (H.L., 1985) Lord Keith said that it was relevant to
consider, in any particular case, whether it would be "just and
reasonable" to impose a duty upon the defendant, but it may be that
this is merely a different way of acknowledging the function of policy.

Recent cases have tended to focus upon the just and reasonable
requirement rather than refer expressly to the second limb of the
Anns test. Thus, in *Jones* v. *Department of Employment* (C.A., 1988)
it was held that it would not be just and reasonable to impose a
common law duty upon an adjudication officer in assessing a claim
for unemployment benefit, given the non-judicial nature of the
officer's functions and the fact that there was a statutory framework
of appeal. Similarly, in *Business Computers International Ltd.* v.
Registrar of Companies (H.C., 1987), where a petition for the
winding-up of a company was served at the wrong address, it was
held that no duty was owed by one litigant to another as to the way
in which the litigation was conducted, since the safeguards against
impropriety were to be found in the rules governing the conduct of
litigation, and not in tort.

There are, of course, numerous relationships which have long been
recognised as giving rise to a duty in law (*e.g.* one road-user and
another, employer and employee), and here no problem arises. It is
in novel cases that the courts may consider the more subtle aspects of
proximity and what is just and reasonable. At the end of the day the
law of negligence is a balancing of competing interests for, as Lord
Pearce observed in *Hedley Byrne & Co. Ltd.* v. *Heller & Partners
Ltd.* (H.L., 1964): "How wide the sphere of the duty of care in
negligence is to be laid depends ultimately on the courts' assessment
of the demands of society for protection from the carelessness of
others." The remainder of this chapter deals with some of the more
well-established areas in which no duty arises in law, or at least
where restrictions are placed upon its scope.

NEGLIGENT MISSTATEMENT: ECONOMIC LOSS

A careless statement upon which the plaintiff relies and which causes
either personal injury or damage to property is actionable in
accordance with ordinary principles (*Clayton* v. *Woodman & Son
(Builders) Ltd.* (H.C., 1962)). In the case of pure economic loss,
however, the courts have been wary lest they create, in the words
of Cardozo C.J. in *Ultramares Corporation* v. *Touche* (1931),
"liability in an indeterminate amount for an indefinite time and
to an indeterminate class." This is an expression of the familiar

"floodgates" argument, namely the fear of opening the way to a proliferation of claims, and of the reluctance to impose upon the defendant a potentially enormous liability out of all proportion to the wrong.

Hedley Byrne v. Heller

Prior to the decision of the House of Lords in *Hedley Byrne & Co. Ltd. v. Heller & Partners Ltd.* (H.L., 1964) liability for statements existed in the tort of deceit and *Derry v. Peek* (H.L., 1889), which finally established that dishonesty was essential to deceit, was interpreted as laying down a rule that there could be no liability in tort in the absence of dishonesty. A duty could arise in equity where the parties were in a fiduciary relationship (see *Nocton v. Lord Ashburton* (H.L., 1914)), and there could, of course, be liability in contract. But in *Candler v. Crane, Christmas & Co.* (C.A., 1951) the traditional view was affirmed that there could be no liability in tort for careless statements.

In *Hedley Byrne* the plaintiffs were advertising agents who wanted to know if they could safely advance credit to their client, X. The plaintiffs' bankers sought references from the defendants, X's bankers, who on two occasions replied, "without responsibility", giving favourable reports. The information was passed to the plaintiffs who suffered financial loss when X went into liquidation. Although X's bankers had indicated that the references were for the private use of the plaintiffs' bankers, they knew that they were required in connection with an advertising contract, and the plaintiffs sued in negligence to recover their loss. It was unanimously held that no duty arose because of the disclaimer, but three of their Lordships thought that, without it, the defendants would have owed a duty. The other two were not prepared to go that far, but considered that there could be situations in which a duty of care would arise. All were agreed that a distinction had to be drawn between words and deeds, primarily because the spoken word is more likely to affect a much wider range of people. Their Lordships spoke of the need for a "special relationship" before a duty would be owed and, although expressed in different ways, it seems that such a relationship will exist whenever the defendant knew or ought reasonably to have foreseen that the plaintiff would rely upon his skill and judgment, and it was reasonable in the circumstances for the plaintiff so to do. If these conditions are satisfied it can be said that the defendant has expressly or impliedly undertaken to exercise care in giving the advice, unless, of course, he has made it plain that his word is not to be relied upon (but see later on the effect of a disclaimer).

Application of Hedley Byrne

The essence of a special relationship in the present context is close proximity and reasonable reliance by the plaintiff, so that "off the cuff" advice given on an informal occasion would not be actionable. Equally, advice given on a purely social occasion will not generally give rise to a duty; but in *Chaudhry* v. *Prabhakar* (C.A., 1988) the Court of Appeal held the defendant liable when he acted negligently as a gratuitous agent in selecting a second-hand car for a friend, although he had conceded that a duty was owed. May L.J., however, thought that the concession was wrongly made and considered that the imposition of a duty in these circumstances would make social regulations and responsibilties between friends unnecessarily hazardous. Even where an opinion is expressed in a business context, it must be clear that the plaintiff is seeking considered advice (*Howard Marine and Dredging Co. Ltd.* v. *A. Ogden & Sons Ltd.* (C.A., 1978)).

A restrictive view was taken by the majority in *Mutual Life and Citizens' Assurance Co. Ltd.* v. *Evatt* (P.C., 1971), where it was held that the defendant had either to be in the business of giving advice of the type sought, or must hold himself out as being possessed of a comparable skill and competence, and as being prepared to take reasonable care. The minority view, however, was that the duty would arise whenever a businessman in the course of his business gave information to a person who let it be known that he was seeking considered advice upon which he intended to act. The English courts have so far favoured the minority view (see, *e.g. Esso Petroleum Co. Ltd.* v. *Mardon* (C.A., 1976)).

The professional adviser such as a banker, accountant, architect, surveyor or lawyer, falls squarely within the *Hedley Byrne* principle, as does the person with a financial interest in the subject-matter of the advice. Thus, in *W.B. Anderson Ltd.* v. *Rhodes (Liverpool) Ltd.* (H.C., 1967) a dealer who acted as a commission agent was held liable when he advised sellers of goods that they could safely extend credit to a company for whom he was acting in the purchase of those goods. Despite observations to the contrary in *Tai Hing Cotton Mill Ltd.* v. *Liu Chong Hing Bank Ltd.* (P.C., 1986), there is substantial authority for the view that the existence of a contract does not preclude the possibility of a concurrent obligation in tort (see, *e.g. Midland Bank Trust Co. Ltd.* v. *Hett, Stubbs and Kemp* (H.C., 1979)). If this view is correct, the plaintiff who pays for his advice may nevertheless be able to sue in tort and thereby avail himself of what could be more advantageous limitation rules regarding the accrual of his cause of action. The duty has certainly been held to apply to pre-contractual negotiations. Thus, in *Esso Petroleum Co. Ltd.* v. *Mardon* (C.A., 1976) a careless statement by the representative of a petrol company to a prospective tenant of their garage as to the potential through-put of petrol was held to be actionable because, apart from the company's financial interest, the information was sought in a business context and the representative, who claimed expertise in the matter, knew or ought to have known that he would be relied upon. The position in such cases is that a person who is induced to contract as a result of a negligent misstatement may either sue in tort or under section 2(1) of the Misrepresentation Act 1967. For the purposes of the statutory claim it is immaterial whether or not the parties are in a special relationship, but the statement must have induced a contract; if it did, section 2(1) has the considerable advantage of shifting the burden to the defendant to prove that he had reasonable grounds for believing, and did in fact believe, that his representation was true (see *Howard Marine & Dredging Co. Ltd.* v. *A. Ogden & Sons Ltd.* (C.A., 1978)). However, a warning note should be sounded, inasmuch as where the parties have seen fit to regulate their rights and obligations by the terms of a contract, there is a marked judicial reluctance to vary, or add to, those terms by imposing a wider obligation in tort (*Reid* v. *Rush & Tompkins Group plc* (C.A., 1989)).

In order for a duty to arise, it seems that some inquiry must be made of the defendant, so that there can be no liability in respect of voluntary statements unasked for by the plaintiff, even if it were intended that reliance should be placed upon them (*Lambert* v. *Lewis* (C.A., 1980)). It need not, however, be the plaintiff who makes the inquiry, provided that, as *Hedley Byrne* itself shows, it is clear that he is a person on whose behalf the information is sought. Alternatively, he may be foreseeable as a member of an identifiable class of persons to whom the information would be given. In *Yianni* v. *Edwin Evans & Sons* (H.C., 1982), for example, a surveyor instructed by a building society to value a house for mortgage purposes was held to owe a duty to the house purchaser (approved in *Smith* v. *Eric S. Bush* (H.L., 1989) and *Harris* v. *Wyre Forest District Council* (H.L., 1989)). Similarly, in *JEB Fasteners Ltd.* v. *Marks, Bloom & Co.* (C.A., 1983) the defendant auditors prepared a company's accounts knowing that the company was in difficulty and was seeking sources of finance, including the possibility of a take-over. Although the audited accounts were not certified with the plaintiffs' eventual take-over specifically in view, the defendants knew of the plaintiffs' interest and ought therefore to have foreseen that they might rely upon those accounts. The duty held to be owed by the auditors appears to have been based on the ordinary foreseeability test, but there was clearly a close degree of proximity between the parties. In the light of recent decisions, foreseeability, proximity and a consideration of what is just and reasonable must all be weighed in the balance, as was recently illustrated in *Caparo Industries plc* v. *Dickman* (C.A., 1989), where it was held that an auditor conducting a statutory audit of a public company owes a duty of care to individual shareholders, but not to investors or potential investors.

It has often been said that the duty in these cases rests upon a "voluntary assumption of responsibility" by the defendant, but, according to Lord Griffiths in *Smith* v. *Bush* this expression is to be understood as referring to the circumstances in which the law will deem the maker of the statement to have assumed responsibility to its recipient. This might explain the imposition of liability where the defendant is under a duty to speak. In *Ministry of Housing and Local Government* v. *Sharp* (C.A., 1970), for example, a local authority was held liable when it issued to an intending purchaser of land a search certificate which negligently omitted a land charge in the plaintiffs' favour with the result that their rights were lost. The Court of Appeal took the view that *Hedley Byrne* was not directly applicable because the plaintiff was a third party in the sense that he was not the person to whom the information was given, nor did he in any way rely upon it. This case was relied upon in *Ross* v. *Caunters* (H.C., 1980) where a solicitor was held liable to an intended beneficiary under a will for failing to inform his client, the testator, that the spouse of a beneficiary should not witness the will. The decision was based upon a straightforward application of *Donoghue* v. *Stevenson* although, as with *JEB Fasteners*, there was a close degree of proximity between the parties and no danger of exposing the defendant to an indeterminate liability. It may now be that whether the plaintiff is the person who actually relied upon the statement, or is a third party, is a matter of little consequence. What is important is that, having satisfied the preliminary requirement of foreseeability of loss to the plaintiff, there is sufficiently close proximity between the parties and the "special relationship" formula of *Hedley Byrne* may simply be regarded as signifying that a closer nexus is needed in the case of negligent words, as distinct from negligent acts.

One final point is whether liability under *Hedley Byrne* can exist in respect of a mere failure to speak. In *Banque Financière de la Cité* v. *Westgate Insurance Co. Ltd.* (C.A., 1989) it was conceded that it could, provided that there was a voluntary assumption of responsibility and reliance thereon, though it would be more difficult to find such an assumption in the case of a mere omission.

Disclaimers and contributory negligence

The decision in *Hedley Byrne* was that no duty was owed because the defendants had effectively excluded liability by stating that they did not accept responsibility. After some initial conflict of authority, the House of Lords in *Smith* v. *Eric S. Bush* (H.L., 1989) and in *Harris* v. *Wyre Forest District Council* (H.L., 1989) has held that such disclaimers are generally caught by section 2(2) of the Unfair Contract Terms Act 1977 and are therefore subject to a test of reasonableness as provided for in section 11(3) of the Act. In both cases surveyors were held to owe a duty of care to prospective mortgagors where the circumstances were such that they knew that the mortgagor had in effect paid for the valuation and would probably rely upon their report. It is worth noting that in *Harris* the duty was held to exist notwithstanding that the mortgagee was a local authority (employing its own "in-house" valuer) statutorily obliged to value the property, and that the mortgage application form stated clearly that the valuation was confidential and solely for the benefit of the council. In their Lordships' opinion sections 11(3) and 13(1) of the 1977 Act supported the view that all exclusion notices which would at common law provide a defence to an action for negligence must satisfy the requirement of reasonableness. Apart from the fact that the purchaser knew that mortgagees were generally trustworthy in appointing professionally competent valuers who were paid for their services at the purchaser's expense, their Lordships said that it had to be borne in mind that, in the case of a typical house purchase, the valuer knew that the majority of buyers in fact relied upon his report and could not afford a second valuation. It was accordingly held that it was unfair and unreasonable for a valuer in these circumstances to rely on an exclusion clause directed against the purchaser, though the House observed that the position might be otherwise where very large sums of money were at stake as, for example, in the case of industrial property or very expensive houses.

In accordance with general principles a disclaimer will be construed *contra proferentem* and must be brought adequately to the plaintiff's notice either before or at the time the statement is made, or at least before he acts in reliance upon it. It is arguable that the existence of a disclaimer of which the plaintiff is aware prevents the duty from arising on the ground that reliance would not be reasonable. However, the *Smith* and *Harris* cases show that this is not necessarily so, especially since section 13(1) of the 1977 Act subjects to the provisions of section 2(2) terms and notices excluding or restricting the obligation or duty, breach of which gives rise to liability. The proper analysis in such a case, therefore, is to determine whether a duty would be owed in the absence of the disclaimer and then, if the answer is yes, apply the 1977 Act. An alternative possibility would be to consider the extent, if any, to which the plaintiff could be said to have caused his own loss and apply the apportionment provisions of the Law Reform (Contributory Negligence) Act 1945 (see Chap. 5). But this approach, too, causes a similar problem in that if the plaintiff's conduct is so unreasonable as to amount to contributory negligence, it is difficult to see how he can be said to have reasonably relied upon the statement. On the issue of causation generally, *JEB Fasteners* serves as a reminder that the plaintiff must prove causation in the usual way so that, unless the statement played "a real and substantial part" in inducing him to act, he must fail.

NEGLIGENT ACTS: ECONOMIC LOSS

Although economic loss consequential upon injury to the person or to property has always been a recoverable item of damage, the law has traditionally been unwilling to entertain claims for "pure" economic loss (see *Cattle* v. *Stockton Waterworks Co.* (H.L., 1875); *Weller & Co.* v. *Foot and Mouth Disease Research Institute* (H.C., 1966)). The distinction between the two types of damage is illustrated in *Spartan Steel & Alloys Ltd.* v. *Martin & Co. (Contractors) Ltd.* (C.A., 1973), where the defendants negligently damaged a power cable, cutting off the electricity supply to the plaintiffs' factory, as a result of which the plaintiffs suffered damage to their property together with loss of profit thereon, and pure loss of profit during the interruption to the supply. The plaintiffs succeeded in respect of the first part of their claim, but failed to recover for loss of profit which they would have made but for the power cut. The avowed justification for restricting the scope of the duty in this type of case is the perennial floodgates argument.

A major inroad upon the principle that damages for economic loss are not generally recoverable in tort was made by *Hedley Byrne*, but the courts continue to distinguish between statements and acts (though the distinction may at times be a fine one). Until recently the law appeared to be moving slowly towards a position where the plaintiff could succeed, provided there was close proximity between the parties and no fear of exposing the defendant to an indeterminate liability (see, *e.g. Ross* v. *Caunters* (H.C., 1980)). In *Dutton* v.

Bognor Regis U.D.C. (C.A., 1972) damages were held to be recoverable by a building owner in respect of damage to the building caused by defective foundations, which had been negligently inspected and approved by the local authority. Lord Denning categorised the loss as physical damage, but the plaintiff was, in reality, being compensated for having received a product of lower quality than she had bargained for, and it had hitherto been accepted that liability only existed for damage to property other than the defective product itself (see Chap. 6). Nevertheless, *Dutton* was approved in *Anns* v. *Merton London Borough Council* (H.L., 1978) where, on similar facts, a local authority was held liable for a negligent exercise of its statutory powers of inspection. Both cases have been explained on the grounds that the defects in the buildings constituted an imminent threat to the health and safety of owners and occupiers, and that compensation was being awarded to cover the cost of averting that threat. Much more radical, however, was the decision in *Junior Books Ltd.* v. *Veitchi Co. Ltd.* (H.L., 1982), where the defendant sub-contractors were nominated by the plaintiffs to lay a floor in their factory and, by reason of alleged defects in the floor, caused economic loss to the plaintiffs. Although the floor did not pose any threat of danger as such, a majority of the House of Lords held that the allegation, if proved, disclosed a good cause of action, because there was a very close relationship of proximity between the parties (falling just short of actual privity of contract) and, as nominated sub-contractors, the defendants must have known that the plaintiffs were relying upon their expertise as flooring specialists.

There is little doubt that *Junior Books* went a considerable way towards recognising a general right of recovery for pure economic loss, but subsequent cases have made it abundantly plain that it establishes no new principle, and is to be confined to its particular facts. In particular, it was held in *Muirhead* v. *Industrial Tank Specialities Ltd.* (C.A., 1985) that the relationship of manufacturer and ultimate consumer is not sufficiently close to enable the consumer to recover economic loss suffered as a result of defects in the quality of goods. Nor has the decision had any effect upon the long-established rule that no claim will lie in respect of foreseeable economic loss, unaccompanied by physical damage to property in which the plaintiff has a proprietary or possessory interest (*Leigh & Sillavan Ltd.* v. *Aliakmon Shipping Co. Ltd.* (H.L., 1986); *Candlewood Navigation Corporation Ltd.* v. *Mitsui OSK Lines Ltd.* (P.C., 1986)). Furthermore, as a challenge to the hallowed belief that questions pertaining essentially to the quality of goods are to be resolved by reference to contractual obligations rather than to tort duties, the life of *Junior Books* has been brief. In *Simaan General Contracting Co.* v. *Pilkington Glass Ltd. (No. 2)* (C.A., 1988) the plaintiff contractors failed in their action against the defendants, who had supplied the wrong type of doube-glazed units to sub-contractors employed to install them, in consequence of which the building owner withheld payments to the plaintiffs. In holding that the parties must have intended that their rights and obligations were to be governed by the various contracts that were made, the Court of Appeal distinguished *Junior Books* on two main grounds. First, it could not be said that the plaintiffs had relied upon the defendants, who were mere suppliers from whom the plaintiffs were obliged to acquire the goods by the terms of their contract with the building owner. Secondly, whilst *Junior Books* had been interpreted as a case involving physical damage, there was no such damage in this case, the alleged "defect" being no more than a failure to comply with implied conditions of correspondence with description and quality in the Sale of Goods Act 1979. The court also adverted to the potential difficulty as to how far exemption clauses or other conditions in the defendants' contract of sale with the sub-contractor might affect the proposed duty in tort to the plaintiffs, who were not privy to that agreement. Dillon L.J. went so far as to say that *Junior Books* had been the subject of so much analysis that future citation from it could not serve any useful purpose. The judicial reluctance to search for a tort duty where the parties have structured their relations by a contractual chain is further illustrated in *Greater Nottingham Co-operative Society Ltd.* v. *Cementation Piling and Foundations Ltd.* (C.A., 1988). The defendant sub-contractors entered into a collateral contract with the plaintiff building owners, the terms of which required the defendants to exercise reasonable care and skill in the design of the works and the selection of materials, but which were silent as to the manner in which the works were to be executed. Following negligent operation of the equipment by the defendants, the plaintiffs suffered economic loss caused by, *inter alia*, the delayed completion of the extension to their building. It was unanimously held that a direct, albeit limited, contractual obligation was inconsistent with any assumption of responsibility beyond that which was expressly undertaken. In other words, the effect of enhancing the close relationship in *Junior Books* by adding a direct contractual bond was to negative, rather than confirm, a duty to avoid economic loss. It would seem to make little difference in this type of case whether the loss is caused by a negligent act or a misstatement (*Pacific Associates Inc.* v. *Baxter* (C.A., 1989)).

The current state of the law in relation to liability for economic loss remains far from clear. It can no longer even be stated with confidence that the *Anns* theory of liability, namely that of awarding damages to avert a "present or imminent danger" to health or safety, continues to apply (in any event, the principle was only ever applied to defective buildings, not other chattels). In *D. & F. Estates Ltd.* v. *Church Commissioners for England* (H.L., 1988) the defendant builders sub-contracted plastering work in the course of building a block of flats. Some 15 years later much of the plaster in the plaintiffs' flat was found to be loose as a result of defective workmanship, and the plaintiffs sued the defendants for the estimated cost of future remedial work, and prospective loss of rent whilst that latter work was carried out. A unanimous House of Lords held that the loss was purely economic and therefore irrecoverable. Lord Bridge concurred with the dissenting judgment of Lord Brandon in *Junior Books* and said that where a latent defect in a chattel or structure was discovered before it had caused either personal injury or damage to other property, the cost of repairing or otherwise eliminating that defect (*e.g.* by demolition) amounted to pure economic loss. Lord Oliver thought that the proposition that tort damages were recoverable for negligent manufacture in relation to defects in, or injury to, the very thing that was manufactured, was peculiar to the construction of a building; but he agreed with Lord Bridge when he said that such a proposition was logically explicable only on the ground that, in the case of a complex structure such as a building, the constituent parts could be treated as separate items of property distinct from that portion of the whole which gave rise to the damage, thus bringing the issue within ordinary *Donoghue* v. *Stevenson* principles. For example, where defective foundations caused cracking in walls and ceilings, the latter could be regarded as "other property" for the purposes of an action; but whereas Lord Oliver considered that damages could be awarded for the cost of the repair to the defective part (*i.e.* the foundations) so far as necessary to repair the damage to the other parts (*i.e.* the walls and ceilings), Lord Bridge doubted whether this was so, because the defective part was not "other property." Furthermore, in contrast to Lord Oliver, Lord Bridge was prepared to extend the "complex structure" analysis to complex chattels. Notwithstanding this decision, the Court of Appeal in *Department of the Environment* v. *Thomas Bates & Son Ltd.* (C.A., 1989) seems to have accepted the traditional *Anns* approach, though the defendant builders were held not liable in this case because there was neither an imminent threat to the health and safety of the occupiers, nor was there damage to property other than the defective component itself.

The law is clearly in a state of uncertainty and it is impossible to formulate a coherent principle of liability in economic loss cases. It is probably the case that policy considerations other than the "indeterminate liability" argument are at stake, though precisely what those considerations are is far from apparent. The perceived, though arguably exaggerated, fear of diluting the supremacy of contractual principles by superimposing tort duties upon a clear contractual chain has also undoubtedly influenced many of the decisions in this area. Little more can be said than that the prevailing judicial inclination is to restrict the expansion of negligence in relation to this type of loss, and each case must therefore be approached in the light of its particular facts.

NERVOUS SHOCK

Where the plaintiff suffers mental distress as a result of his personal injuries, the law may take account of it in the assessment of damages for pain and suffering. But "shock" in the present context is used to signify some recognisable medical condition, whether physical or psychiatric, brought about not by any direct physical impact, but by what the plaintiff has seen or heard (or possibly read); mere grief or emotional distress is not sufficient. The courts were originally wary of admitting such claims, partly for fear of encouraging a proliferation of claims (some possibly fraudulent, at least when the study of psychiatry was in its infancy), and partly in the belief that there were increased evidentiary difficulties tending to protracted litigation. In *Dulieu* v. *White* (H.C., 1901) the plaintiff could recover when she reasonably feared for her own safety as a result of the defendant's negligence, and the principle was extended in *Hambrook* v. *Stokes Bros.* (C.A., 1925) to a plaintiff who reasonably feared for the safety of loved ones, in this case her children. It came to be accepted that the test of liability was reasonable foreseeability of injury by shock, though what could be regarded as foreseeable was circumscribed by two factors. First, the shock had to be the result of what the plaintiff perceived by his own unaided senses (*Hambrook* v. *Stokes Bros.*); secondly, with one or two notable exceptions (*e.g. Chadwick* v. *British Transport Commission* (C.A., 1967), where a rescuer assisting at the scene of a train crash was held entitled to recover), it seemed that the plaintiff had, as a rule, to be related in some way to the immediate victim of the defendant's negligence.

The law is now to be found in *McLoughlin* v. *O'Brian* (H.L., 1982), where the defendant negligently caused an accident in which two of the plaintiff's children and her husband were seriously injured, and another daughter killed. The plaintiff was at home at the time and first heard of the accident from a friend who drove her to the hospital to which her family had been taken. She there learned of her daughter's death and saw her husband and two children in circumstances which were "capable of producing an effect going well beyond that of grief and sorrow." The House of Lords held that shock was reasonably foreseeable and unanimously allowed the plaintiff's claim. Lord Wilberforce, with whom Lord Edmund-Davies agreed, thought that, as a matter of policy, there had to be some restriction on the duty of care, based upon the nature of the tie or relationship between the plaintiff and the victim (the closer the tie, the greater the claim for consideration), the proximity of the plaintiff to the accident in time and space, and the means by which the shock was caused, which would exclude from consideration those whose shock was attributable to what they were told by a third party. Lords Bridge and Scarman, on the other hand, advocated a test based upon foreseeability alone and, whilst accepting that the criteria suggested by Lord Wilberforce might have a bearing on whether shock was foreseeable in any given case, they did not think that those criteria placed a legal limitation upon the plaintiff's right of recovery. Lord Russell, too, adopted a test of reasonable foreseeability, but gave no indication as to how the test should be applied; like his brethren, he expressly rejected the floodgates argument on the basis that the number of successful claims was likely to be small, although he intimated that policy might be relevant in an appropriate case.

Whilst not altogether clear, it is at least arguable that liability for shock is now based exclusively upon a test of reasonable foresight. It must no doubt continue to be assumed that the plaintiff is a person of ordinary fortitude who is not abnormally susceptible to shock (see *Bourhill* v. *Young* (H.L., 1943)). But if shock to a person of normal fortitude is foreseeable, the "thin skull" principle (see Chap. 4) will enable one who is particularly susceptible to recover for the full extent of his injuries, even though exacerbated by a predisposition to psychiatric disorder (*Brice* v. *Brown* (H.C., 1984)). In *Attia* v. *British Gas plc* (C.A., 1988) the plaintiff allegedly suffered shock upon witnessing the destruction of her home in a fire caused by the defendants' negligence. On a preliminary issue it was held that there was no principle of law to the effect that shock resulting from damage to property could never be regarded as foreseeable, and the action was ordered to be tried.

LEGAL IMMUNITIES

By contrast with the solicitor-client relationship, no contract exists between a barrister and his client, and this was for long thought to be justification for the rule that a barrister could not be liable in negligence to his client. Following *Hedley Byrne* such an argument was no longer tenable, and in *Rondel* v. *Worsley* (H.L., 1969) the House of Lords (in holding that an advocate, whether barrister or solicitor, did not owe a duty to his client in respect of the way in which a case was conducted in court) sought to justify the immunity principally upon the policy ground that, in order to fulfil his duty to the court and to the administration of justice, the advocate had to be free from the threat of negligence actions by dissatisfied clients. In *Saif Ali* v. *Sydney Mitchell & Co.* (H.L., 1980) the immunity was extended to encompass pre-trial work which is so intimately connected with the conduct of the cause in court that it can fairly be said to be a preliminary decision affecting the way that the cause is to be conducted at the hearing. In *Somasundaram* v. *M. Julius Melchior & Co.* (C.A., 1989) the view was taken that advice as to a plea in a criminal case fell within the immunity, but that, as regards solicitors, such immunity protected them only *qua* advocates and not where counsel was engaged. The precise scope of the immunity is unclear, but it extends to claims against an advocate by opposing parties in civil litigation (*Orchard* v. *South Eastern Electricity Board* (H.C., 1987)) although, on the rather exceptional facts of *Al-Kandari* v. *J.R. Brown & Co.* (C.A., 1988), it did not protect a solicitor who stepped outside his role as representative simply for his client and who also assumed responsibilities towards his client's opponent. A further policy argument advanced in *Rondel* v. *Worsley* in support of the immunity was that an action against the advocate would involve a retrial of the issues which arose in the original case, but this would, according to *Hunter* v. *Chief Constable of West Midlands Police* (H.L., 1981), now appear to operate as an independent bar. Thus, in *Somasundaram* it was held that, even if the advocate was not immune within the *Saif Ali* principle, he still could not be sued if those proceedings would amount to impugning, either directly or indirectly, a decision on the merits by a court of competent jurisdiction, since to allow such an action would be an abuse of process and contrary to public policy.

Apart from advocates, certain others, including judges, those exercising a quasi-judicial function, and witnesses, have a wide immunity from actions in tort, avowedly in recognition of the public interest in the due administration of justice. So, too, a litigant does not owe a duty of care to an opponent as to the manner in which the litigation is conducted, because the safeguards against impropriety are to be found in the rules and procedures governing the conduct of litigation, and not in tort (*Business Computers International Ltd.* v. *Registrar of Companies* (H.C., 1987)). For reasons of policy which are similar to the above, the police function of conducting an investigation does not give rise to a duty of care either to an individual member of the public (*Hill* v. *Chief Constable of West Yorkshire* (H.L., 1988)) or to the subject of that investigation (*Calveley* v. *Chief Constable of the Merseyside Police* (H.L., 1989)).

INJURY BY THIRD PARTIES

Where the plaintiff suffers damage as a result of the defendant's negligence and, some time later, further damage is caused by the independent act of a third party, which would not have been caused but for the original negligence, the issue is whether the third party's conduct breaks the chain of causation (see Chap. 4). Where, however, the only damage suffered is attributable to the wrongdoing of the independent actor, the defendant's potential liability is determined, usually by a consideration of the scope of the duty owed. As a general proposition it can be stated that even if A is at fault, he is not liable for damage to C which B deliberately chooses to do (*Weld-Blundell* v. *Stephens* (H.L., 1920)). The defendant will be liable, however, if he stands in a special relationship to the third party such that he has a duty to control the conduct of the third party in order to prevent damage to the plaintiff. Examples of such relationships include Borstal officer and trainee (*Home Office* v. *Dorset Yacht Co. Ltd.* (H.L., 1970)), parent and child (*Newton* v. *Edgerley* (C.A., 1959)), and employer and employee (*Hudson* v. *Ridge Manufacturing Co. Ltd.* (H.C., 1957)). This is not so say that a parent, for example, will always be responsible for the torts of his child, but simply that there are situations where he is under a duty to take reasonable care to see that his child does not cause foreseeable injury. Similarly the defendant may stand in a particular relationship to the plaintiff such that a positive duty is imposed upon him to prevent harm (*e.g.* occupier and visitor; see Chap. 8).

More difficult are those cases where the defendant does not stand in any particular relationship either with the third party or the plaintiff. Here, the defendant may still be held to owe a duty if, by his conduct, he creates a foreseeable risk that the third party may intervene, but the difficulty is in determining the precise circumstances in which the duty will arise and, if so, the scope of that duty.

In *P. Perl (Exporters) Ltd.* v. *Camden London Borough Council* (C.A., 1983) the defendants were held not liable when thieves entered their premises and thereby gained access to, and stole from, the plaintiffs' neighbouring property, since they were under no duty to secure their premises in order to restrain that type of activity. On the other hand, in *Dove* v. *Banham's Patent Locks Ltd.* (C.A., 1983) burglary prevention specialists were held liable when, as a result of their failure to install a security gate properly, burglars broke in and stole from the plaintiffs. The two cases are readily distinguishable on the ground that, in *Dove*, theft from the plaintiff's premises was the very risk which the defendants had originally been employed to avert.

The whole question of liability for wilful wrongdoing was considered by the House of Lords in *Smith* v. *Littlewoods Organisation Ltd.* (H.L., 1987) where the defendants bought a disused cinema with the intention of demolishing it to make way for a supermarket. While the premises were empty, vandals gained access and, on at least two occasions, attempts were made to start a fire, though neither the defendants nor the police had been informed. Eventually a fire was started which spread and caused damage to the plaintiffs' adjacent property. The plaintiffs' claim was unanimously rejected. Lord Goff said that there was no general duty of care to prevent a third party from causing damage to the plaintiff by deliberate wrongdoing, however foreseeable such harm might be, because the common law does not normally impose liability for pure omissions. There could be liability, he said, where the defendant is responsible for controlling the third party (see above), or where he negligently causes or permits to be created a source of danger, and it is reasonably foreseeable that third parties may interfere with it and thereby cause damage (as in *Haynes* v. *Harwood* (C.A., 1935)); or where he fails to abate a known risk created by third parties upon his property (*cf. Goldman* v. *Hargrave* (P.C., 1967); see Chap. 11). None of these circumstances applied to *Smith's* case, however, because the defendants were unaware of the presence of the vandals, and the risk was therefore not foreseeable. Lords Brandon and Griffiths said that the duty owed by the defendants was to take reasonable care to ensure that the cinema was not, and did not become, a source of danger to neighbouring occupiers, but since there was nothing inherently dangerous on the premises, and because the defendants did not know of the vandals' activities, the risk was unforeseeable. Lord Mackay, too, adopted the test of reasonable foresight, but indicated that there might be circumstances where the risk would have to be "highly likely" before it could be regarded as reasonably foreseeable; in this case, he said, whilst it was probable that persons might attempt to enter the vacant premises, it was by no means a probable consequence of the vacation of those premises that they would be set on fire.

CHAPTER 3

NEGLIGENCE: BREACH OF DUTY

THE REASONABLE MAN

Once it is established that the defendant owed to the particular plaintiff a duty of care, it must then be proved that the defendant was in breach of duty. Negligence was defined in *Blyth* v. *Birmingham Waterworks Co.* (Ex., 1856) as "the omission to do something which a reasonable man, guided upon those considerations which ordinarily regulate the conduct of human affairs, would do, or doing something which a prudent and reasonable man would not do." As a matter of law, therefore, the standard of care required of the defendant is that of the hypothetical, reasonable man and, whilst no man is expected to attain perfection, that standard is objective in the sense that it generally takes no account of the idiosyncrasies of the person whose conduct is in question (*Glasgow Corporation* v. *Muir* (H.L., 1943)). However, whether the defendant has reached the required standard in any given case is a question of fact, so that previous decisions should not be relied upon as precedents for what constitutes negligence.

The standard of reasonable care is therefore invariable in the sense that the law does not recognise differing degrees of negligence, but it is an infinitely flexible concept enabling the court in any given situation to impose standards ranging from very low to very high. For example, the standard required of a participant in a competitive sport *vis-à-vis* spectators and fellow players may be described as low (see, *e.g. Wooldridge* v. *Sumner* (C.A., 1963)). Conversely, standards imposed on motorists fall little short of a counsel of perfection, and the Court of Appeal in *Nettleship* v. *Weston* (C.A., 1971) held that the learner driver must exercise the skill of a reasonably competent, experienced driver. The imposition of such high standards may be justified where the defendant is engaged in a high-risk activity, and there can be little doubt that, in some instances, compulsory liability insurance has influenced the court in fixing the level of care.

THE CONCEPT OF RISK

What is reasonable conduct varies with the particular circumstances, and liability depends ultimately on what the reasonable man would have foreseen. However, whilst the defendant is not negligent if the consequences of his conduct were unforeseeable, it does not necessarily follow that he will be liable for all foreseeable consequences. In practice the courts evaluate the defendant's behaviour in terms of risk, so that he will be adjudged negligent if he exposes the plaintiff to an unreasonable risk of harm. To this end a number of factors must be weighed in the balance, including the magnitude of the risk, the social utility or desirability (if any) of the activity in question, and the cost and practicability of precautionary measures to minimise or eliminate the risk. In performing this balancing act the court will decide what weight is to be given to each of these factors and will make a value judgment as to what the reasonable man would have done in the circumstances.

Magnitude of the risk

The degree of care which the law exacts must be commensurate with the risk created. Two factors are involved here, namely the likelihood that harm will be caused and the potential gravity of that harm should the risk materialise. In *Bolton* v. *Stone* (H.L., 1951) the plaintiff was standing in the road when she was struck by a cricket ball which had been hit out of the defendants' ground. There was evidence that this had happened six times in the preceding 30 years, so the risk was one of which the defendants were aware and which was therefore foreseeable. Nevertheless the defendants were held not liable because the risk was so small that they were justified in not taking further measures to eliminate it.

The relevance of the potential gravity of the consequences is illustrated in *Paris* v. *Stepney B.C.* (H.L., 1951) where a one-eyed garage worker became totally blind after being struck in the eye by a metal chip which flew from a bolt which he was trying to hammer loose. The defendant employers were held liable for failing to provide him with safety goggles, even though they were justified in not providing such equipment to a person with normal sight. Although the risk was small, the injury to this particular plaintiff was very serious.

The degree of risk to which the plaintiff is exposed will also depend, as is evident from *Paris*, upon any physical abnormality from which he may suffer so that, if such abnormality is or ought to be known to the defendant, that is a factor which must be taken into account. Thus, if a hole is dug in the pavement adequate steps must be taken to prevent blind people from falling into it (*Haley* v. *London Electricity Board* (H.L., 1965)). A disability of which the defendant could not reasonably have known is obviously irrelevant and, in this connection, there is no duty upon an employer to ensure that his employee is literate (*James* v. *Hepworth & Grandage Ltd.* (C.A., 1968)).

Social utility

The purpose to be served, if sufficiently important or desirable, may justify the assumption of what might otherwise be regarded as an abnormal risk. In *Watt* v. *Hertfordshire C.C.* (C.A., 1954), for example, a fireman was injured by the movement of a heavy jack whilst travelling in a lorry which was not properly equipped to carry it. The jack was urgently needed to save the life of a woman who had become trapped under a bus, and the defendants were accordingly held to be justified in exposing the plaintiff to that risk. On the other hand, the laudable object of saving human life or limb has its limits and is plainly self-defeating if the danger risked is too great, so that a fire authority has been held negligent where a fire engine passed through a red traffic signal on its way to a fire and caused a collision (*Ward* v. *L.C.C.* (H.C., 1938)).

Cost of precautions

The risk has to be weighed against the cost and practicability of minimising or overcoming it. In *Latimer* v. *A.E.C. Ltd.* (H.L., 1953) a factory floor became slippery with oil and water after a heavy rainfall caused flooding. Despite taking such steps as they were able, the defendants could not entirely eradicate the danger and the plaintiff slipped and was injured. The defendants were held not liable because the risk was not so great as to require the drastic step of closing the factory until the floor dried out.

CHARACTERISTICS OF THE DEFENDANT

It has already been noted that the legal standard generally takes no account of the personal characteristics of the particular defendant, who cannot therefore be heard to say that he did his incompetent best. Inexperience or lack of intelligence or slow reactions provide no excuse to a charge of negligence. Nor, for that matter, will a defendant be able to avail himself of some lower standard on account of his physical disability. A partially sighted driver owes the same duty as one with normal sight, and the fact that he has a reduced field of vision merely imposes upon him an obligation to proceed with greater caution. The reasonable man is expected to know those things that common experience teaches and, in appropriate cases, he can be expected to anticipate that others may be careless. Two types of defendant, children and those professing a particular skill, require special mention.

Children

As far as children are concerned, there is no defence of minority as such and a child is as responsible for his torts (through his guardian *ad litem*) as a person of full age. Thus, a boy of 16 has been held negligent in the use of an air rifle (*Gorely* v. *Codd* (H.C., 1967)). But, by analogy with the approach adopted in cases of contributory negligence (see Chap. 5), his age will be relevant in determining whether he is capable of the necessary mental state, and he will, it seems, be judged in accordance with standards of behaviour to be reasonably expected of a child of his age. Where a young child does cause injury by conduct which in an adult would be classed as negligent then, more often than not, a parent or other responsible person, such as a teacher, will be liable. This is not a vicarious liability but a primary liability arising from a failure to exercise proper supervision and control (*Carmarthenshire C.C.* v. *Lewis* (H.L., 1955)).

Professionals

A person who holds himself out as having a particular skill or profession must attain the standard of the reasonably competent man exercising that skill or profession. The level of skill demanded, however, will vary according to the extent of the risk. For example, the do-it-yourself enthusiast fixing a door handle in his home must reach the standard of a reasonably competent carpenter doing that type of work, but not of a professional working for reward (*Wells* v. *Cooper* (C.A., 1958)). If, however, the work is of a technical or complex nature, and there is a risk of serious injury should it not be properly done, the defendant may be expected either to employ an expert or to display the same degree of skill.

A member of a profession discharges his duty by conforming to the standards of a reasonably competent member of that profession and inexperience is no excuse. Thus, a doctor must act in accordance with a practice accepted as proper by a body of responsible and skilled medical opinion, and is not negligent merely because there is a body of opinion which would take a contrary view. This was the test laid down in *Bolam* v. *Friern Barnet Hospital Management Committee* (H.C., 1957), and indeed it has since been held that where there is more than one accepted method of doing things, both or all of which are regarded as proper by a skilled body of opinion, the judge is not entitled to make a finding of negligence on the basis of his preference for one method rather than another (*Maynard* v. *West Midlands Regional Health Authority* (H.L., 1984)). The duty of the doctor is the same whether the matter be one of treatment, diagnosis or advice (*Sidaway* v. *Governors of the Bethlem Royal Hospital* (H.L., 1985)). Although the *Bolam* test applies to professions generally, it has on occasions been interpreted, in relation only to the medical profession, to mean that practitioners themselves are the final arbiters in determining standards of professional competence. It is clear, however, that this is not so (see, *e.g.* *Gold* v. *Haringey Health Authority* (C.A., 1987)), although the effect of the test is undoubtedly to make proof of professional negligence extremely difficult where the defendant has followed an accepted practice.

An error of judgment by a professional may or may not be negligent, depending upon whether it was such as a reasonably competent practitioner might make (*Whitehouse* v. *Jordan* (H.L., 1981)). Finally, it is part of the professional's duty to keep abreast of new developments and techniques, as what is reasonably foreseeable may depend upon the state of existing knowledge within that profession at the time. Thus, in *Roe* v. *Minister of Health* (C.A., 1954) an anaesthetist was not negligent in failing to appreciate the risk of percolation of a preservative through invisible cracks in glass ampoules in which the anaesthetic was stored, because such a danger was not known to exist at the time.

EVIDENCE OF NEGLIGENCE

It is for the plaintiff to prove, on a balance of probabilities, that the defendant was negligent. Conformity to general practice is generally regarded as evidence that reasonable care has been taken, but this is not conclusive (*Cavanagh* v. *Ulster Weaving Co. Ltd.* (H.L., 1960)) although as indicated above in the case of professionals who have so conformed, negligence is very difficult to establish. Conversely, failure to conform to approved practice is evidence that there is negligence and requires justification (*Clark* v. *MacLennan* (H.C.,

1983)) but again it is not conclusive of the matter (*Brown* v. *Rolls Royce Ltd.* (H.L., 1960)).

In order to discharge the burden of proof the plaintiff must usually prove particular conduct on the part of the defendant which can be regarded as negligent. He will not be able to do so, however, if he does not know how the accident was caused and, in such a case, he may be able to rely on the maxim *res ipsa loquitur* (the thing speaks for itself). This is simply a rule of evidence by which the plaintiff, who is unable to explain how the accident happened, asks the court to make a prima facie finding of negligence which it is then for the defendant to rebut if he can. After a long history of uncertainty on the issue, the Privy Council has now held that there is no shift in the legal burden of proof (*Ng Chun Pui* v. *Lee Chuen Tat* (P.C., 1988)). There are three conditions necessary for the application of the doctrine according to *Scott* v. *London and St. Katherine Docks Co.* (E.C., 1865); there must be an absence of explanation as to how the accident happened, the "thing" which causes the damage must be under the control of the defendant (or someone for whose negligence he is responsible), and the accident must be such as would not ordinarily occur without negligence.

With regard to the first requirement, if the cause of the accident is known the doctrine does not apply because all that need then be done is to decide whether, on the facts, negligence is proved (*Barkway* v. *South Wales Transport Co. Ltd.* (H.L., 1950)). The operation of the second requirement is illustrated in *Easson* v. *L.N.E.R.* (C.A., 1944) where it was held that the doors of a long distance express train could not be said to be under the continuous control of the defendants, so that a child who fell out of the train could not rely on the maxim. Control by the defendant depends on the probability of outside interference. If the facts establish that such interference was improbable, the defendant will be regarded as being in control.

Whether the accident is such as would not ordinarily have happened without negligence is to be judged in the light of common experience. Thus the maxim has been applied where a plaintiff went into hospital with two stiff fingers and came out with four stiff fingers (*Cassidy* v. *Ministry of Health* (C.A., 1951)), to an unexplained and violent skid in a vehicle (*Richley* v. *Faull* (H.C., 1965)), and on a number of occasions to foreign substances found in consumer products (*Grant* v. *Australian Knitting Mills Ltd.* (P.C., 1936)). In *Ward* v. *Tesco Stores Ltd.* (C.A., 1976) it was held to apply where the plaintiff slipped on some yoghurt on a supermarket floor but, in view of the absence of evidence as to how long the yoghurt had been there, the decision seems doubtful.

If the maxim applies (and it need not be specifically pleaded) the defendant may be able to rebut the inference of negligence if he can show how the accident actually occurred, and that explanation is consistent with no negligence on his part, or he may be able to provide a reasonable explanation of how the accident could have happened without negligence, in which case one of the essential conditions for the application of the maxim is not satisfied. It must, however, be a reasonable explanation and not merely a theoretical possibility because, one way or another, the defendant must show that he was not negligent, and the burden upon him may be very onerous, particularly where there is a high risk of serious harm (*Henderson* v. *H.E. Jenkins & Sons* (H.L., 1970)).

CHAPTER 4

NEGLIGENCE: DAMAGE

The plaintiff must prove that his damage was caused by the defendant's breach, both as a matter of fact and as a matter of law. If as a matter of law the breach is not regarded as causing the damage, it is usually said that the damage is too remote.

FACTUAL CAUSATION

In determining whether the defendant's breach is a cause of the damage in fact it is usual to employ the "but-for" test which enables the court to reject those factors which could not have had any causal effect. "If the damage would not have happened but for a particular fault then that fault is the cause of the damage; if it would have happened just the same, fault or no fault, the fault is not the cause of the damage" (*per* Denning L.J. in *Cork* v. *Kirby Maclean Ltd.* (C.A., 1952)). In *Barnett* v. *Chelsea & Kensington Hospital Management Committee* (H.C., 1969) the failure of a casualty officer to examine a patient, who later died of arsenic poisoning, was held not to have been a cause of death because evidence showed that the patient would probably have died in any event. The "but-for" test will not, however, always solve the problem as is apparent where two

simultaneous wrongs are done to the plaintiff, each of which would in
itself be sufficient to cause the damage. In this case the test leads to
the absurd result that neither breach is a cause of the damage,
whereas in practice both will be held to have caused it.

Since the burden of proof is upon the plaintiff to prove, on a
balance of probabilities, that the breach of duty caused the damage,
difficulties may arise where the precise cause of the damage is
unknown. In *McGhee* v. *National Coal Board* (H.L., 1973) the
plaintiff, who came into contact with abrasive dust as part of his
normal employment, contracted dermatitis and alleged that it was due
to the defendants' failure to provide facilities for washing after work.
The plaintiff succeeded on the ground that it was sufficient to show
that the defendants' breach materially increased the risk of injury,
even though medical knowledge at the time was unable to establish
the breach as the probable cause. This decision had potentially far-
reaching effects, particularly for cases of medical negligence, and an
attempt was made at first instance in *Hotson* v. *East Berkshire Area
Health Authority* (H.L., 1987) to extend the principle so as to impose
liability in respect of the loss of a chance of recovery. The plaintiff
injured his hip in a fall and, as a result of negligent medical
diagnosis, suffered a permanent deformity the risk of which would,
had proper treatment been given, have been reduced by 25 per cent.
The trial judge's decision to award that percentage of the loss was
upheld in the Court of Appeal but reversed by the House of Lords
on the ground that the plaintiff had not proved his case on a balance
of probabilities. Had he been able to do so, their Lordships made it
clear that there was no principle of law which would have justified a
discount from the full measure of damages, incidentally demonstrat-
ing that, ignoring any possibility of contributory negligence, the
plaintiff's claim is determined on an "all or nothing" basis. Any
suggestion that *McGhee's* case establishes a new principle was
decisively rejected by the House of Lords in *Wilsher* v. *Essex Area
Health Authority* (H.L., 1988), where their Lordships simply said that
the court in *McGhee* had properly concluded that the breach of duty
had materially contributed to the injury.

The position becomes more complex where successive acts cause
damage. In *Baker* v. *Willoughby* (H.L., 1970) the plaintiff's leg was
injured through the defendant's negligence, and some time later,
before the trial of the action, he was shot during a robbery in the
same leg which then had to be amputated. It was held that the
plaintiff's right of recovery was not limited to the loss suffered only
before the date of the robbery, but that he was entitled to the
damages that he would have received had there been no subsequent

injury. By contrast, in *Jobling* v. *Associated Dairies Ltd.* (H.L., 1980) the defendant's negligence caused a reduction in the plaintiff's earning capacity. Three years later, but before trial the plaintiff was found to be suffering from a complaint, wholly unrelated to the original accident, which totally incapacitated him. The defendants were held liable only for the loss up to the time of the plaintiff's disablement. In *Baker* the later act was tortious whereas in *Jobling* it was a natural event, but the distinction is not very compelling. The decision in the former case is perhaps justifiable on the ground that to have applied the "but-for" test in its full rigour would have left the plaintiff under-compensated. For even had the robbers been sued to judgment, they would have been liable only for depriving the plaintiff of an already damaged leg.

REMOTENESS OF DAMAGE

It is not for every consequence of the defendant's wrong that the plaintiff is entitled to compensation. In order to contain the defendant's liability within reasonable bounds a line must be drawn, and those consequences which fall on the far side of that line are said to be too remote or, to put the matter another way, are regarded as not having been caused in law by the defendant's breach of duty.

Competing tests

In *Re Polemis* (C.A., 1921) a ship's cargo of benzine had leaked filling the hold with inflammable vapour. Stevedores unloading the vessel negligently dropped a plank into the hold, and the defendant employers were held liable for the destruction of the ship in the ensuing blaze because that loss was a direct, albeit unforeseeable, consequence of the negligence. Whilst not denying the relevance of foreseeability to the existence of a duty, the case did decide that it was not relevant in determining for what consequences the defendant should pay.

This approach was, however, disapproved by the Privy Council in *The Wagon Mound* (P.C., 1961), which substituted a test of reasonable foresight of consequence for that of directness. The defendants negligently discharged into Sydney Harbour a large quantity of fuel oil which drifted to the plaintiffs' wharf where welding was in progress. The plaintiffs discontinued their operations, but later resumed following an assurance that the oil was in no danger of igniting. A fire did eventually break out, however, causing damage to the plaintiffs' wharf and to two ships upon which work was being done. It was found as a fact that some damage to the wharf was reasonably foreseeable by way of fouling of the slipway but that, in view of expert evidence, it was unforeseeable that the oil would ignite. The defendants were accordingly held not liable.

A number of points may be noted here. First, the courts have come to accept *The Wagon Mound* as representing the law. Secondly, the foreseeability of an event and the likelihood or otherwise of its occurring are quite different matters, and whilst the latter may be relevant to the issue of breach of duty (see Chap. 3), the degree of foresight is generally irrelevant to the question of remoteness (see, however, the section in this Chapter on intervening acts). Thus, in *The Wagon Mound (No. 2)* (P.C., 1967) an action brought by the owners of the vessels damaged in the fire succeeded because it was found as a fact, on different evidence, that although the risk of fire was very slight, it was nonetheless foreseeable. Thirdly, although *The Wagon Mound (No. 2)* held that foreseeability was the test for remoteness in cases of nuisance also it is unclear how far, if at all, the principle applies to other torts. It would appear not to apply where the defendant intends to cause injury because that "disposes of any question of remoteness" (*Quinn* v. *Leathem* (H.L., 1901)), but whether torts of strict liability are governed by foreseeability is a matter of controversy. Finally, the general tendency is to adopt a liberal approach to foreseeability, so that neither the extent of the harm nor the precise manner of its infliction need be foreseeable, provided it falls broadly within a foreseeable class of damage. Taken in conjunction with the "egg-shell skull" principle, this means that, in practice, the same result would often be achieved whichever of the competing tests is applied.

Manner of occurrence

In *Hughes* v. *Lord Advocate* (H.L., 1963) post office employees negligently left a manhole uncovered with a canvas shelter over it, surrounded by paraffin lamps. The plaintiff, aged eight, took one of the lamps into the shelter and knocked it into the manhole. By an unusual combination of circumstances there was a violent explosion in which the boy was badly burned. Although the explosion was unforeseeable, the defendants were held liable because burns from the lamp were foreseeable, and it was immaterial that the precise chain of events leading to the injury was not. So too, in *Wieland* v. *Cyril Lord Carpets Ltd.* (H.C., 1969) the plaintiff recovered when, as a result of an injury caused by the defendants' negligence, she could not adjust to the wearing of her spectacles and later fell down some steps sustaining further injury. By way of contrast, in *Doughty* v. *Turner Manufacturing Co. Ltd.* (C.A., 1964) the defendants' employee dropped an asbestos cover into a vat of molten liquid which, due to an unforeseeable chemical reaction, erupted and burned a fellow worker standing nearby. It was held that, even if injury by splashing were foreseeable (which was doubted), the eruption was not, and the plaintiff failed. This case is clearly at odds with *Hughes*, because if it is accepted that some injury by burning was foreseeable, then it ought not to matter that the way in which it occurred was not. On the balance of authority *Hughes* is to be preferred.

Type of damage

The precise nature of the damage need not be foreseeable, provided it is of a type which could have been foreseen. The difficulty in defining damage "of a type" is illustrated by two contrasting cases. In *Bradford* v. *Robinson Rentals Ltd.* (H.C., 1967) a van driver sent on a long journey in an unheated vehicle in severe weather was able to recover for frostbite because, although not in itself foreseeable, it was within the broad class of foreseeable risk arising from exposure to extreme cold. In *Tremain* v. *Pike* (H.C., 1969) the defendant's alleged negligence caused his farm to become rat-infested with the result that the plaintiff contracted a rare disease by contact with rat's urine. It was held that, even if negligence had been proved, the plaintiff could not succeed because although injury from rat bites or food contamination was foreseeable, this particularly rare disease was entirely different in kind. The decision in *Bradford* is a more accurate reflection of the current tendency to adopt a liberal approach to this issue.

Extent of damage; the "egg-shell skull" rule

Subject to what has been said above, it matters not that the actual damage is far greater in extent than could have been foreseen. Thus, in *Vacwell Engineering Co. Ltd.* v. *B.D.H. Chemicals Ltd.* (C.A., 1971) the plaintiffs purchased a chemical manufactured and supplied by the defendants, who failed to give warning that it was liable to cause a minor explosion upon contact with water. The plaintiffs' employee placed a large quantity of the chemical in a sink whereupon an explosion of unforeseeable violence extensively damaged the premises. Since the explosion and consequent damage were foreseeable, even though the magnitude and extent thereof were not, the defendants were held liable.

A similar rule operates where the plaintiff suffers foreseeable personal injury which is exacerbated by some pre-existing physical or psychic abnormality. This so-called "egg-shell skull" principle survives

The Wagon Mound (P.C., 1961) and imposes liability upon the defendant for harm which is not only greater in extent than, but which is of an entirely different kind to, that which is foreseeable. In *Smith* v. *Leech Brain & Co. Ltd.* (H.C., 1962) a workman who had a predisposition to cancer received a burn on the lip from molten metal due to a colleague's negligence. The defendants were held liable for his eventual death from cancer triggered off by the burn. The principle applies equally to a plaintiff who suffers from nervous shock (*Brice* v. *Brown* (H.C., 1984)) and to one with an "egg-shell personality" (*Malcolm* v. *Broadhurst* (H.C., 1970)). Thus, in *Meah* v. *McCreamer* (H.C., 1985) the plaintiff underwent a marked personality change brought about by injuries received in a collision for which the defendant was responsible. This led him to commit a number of serious assaults culminating in a life sentence, and he recovered damages for the deprivation of his liberty. In *Robinson* v. *Post Office* (C.A., 1974) the principle was applied to a plaintiff who suffered serious damage due to an allergy to medical treatment, which was foreseeably required as a result of an injury caused by the defendants' negligence.

According to *Liesbosch Dredger* v. *S.S. Edison* (H.L., 1933) the "egg-shell skull" rule does not apply where the plaintiff's loss is aggravated by his own lack of financial resources. The distinction between physical or psychic peculiarities on the one hand, and lack of means on the other, appears to have no basis in logic and may be a matter of policy. Nor is it clear where the line is to be drawn between *The Liesbosch* and the plaintiff's duty to mitigate his loss. In the latter case the plaintiff's impecuniosity may be a relevant factor in determining whether he has acted reasonably (*Dodd Properties (Kent) Ltd.* v. *Canterbury City Council* (C.A., 1980)), and it is worth noting that whilst the burden rests upon the plaintiff to show that his loss is not too remote, it is upon the defendant to show that the plaintiff failed to act reasonably in mitigation. There have been attacks upon *The Liesbosch* but, notwithstanding attempts to circumvent it, it is still applied (see, *e.g. Ramwade Ltd.* v. *J.W. Emson & Co. Ltd.* (C.A., 1987)). In *Dodd Properties* the plaintiffs were able to convince the court that their delay in effecting repairs to their negligently-damaged property was based upon sound commercial sense rather than a lack of resources, and it was therefore held that they were entitled to the higher cost of repairs at the date of trial. Indeed it is arguable that the rule ought never to apply in the case of damage to non-profit-earning property so long as liability remains in dispute (see *Perry* v. *Sidney Phillips & Son* (C.A., 1982)). It is clear that the uncertainty as to the precise status of *The Liesbosch* is in urgent need of resolution by the House of Lords.

INTERVENING CAUSES

In some cases the plaintiff's damage is alleged to be attributable not to the defendant's breach of duty, but to some intervening event which breaks the chain of causation. Such an event is called a *novus actus interveniens* and is usually dealt with as part of the issue of remoteness because even though the damage would not have occurred "but for" the defendant's breach, it may still be regarded in law as falling outside the scope of the risk created by the original fault.

Plaintiff's intervention

In *McKew* v. *Holland & Hannen & Cubitts (Scotland) Ltd.* (H.L., 1969) the plaintiff's leg would give way without warning as a result of an injury caused by the defendants' negligence. Whilst descending a steep flight of steps without assistance or support, his leg gave way and he fell and fractured his ankle. The defendants were held not liable for this further injury because, although foreseeable, the plaintiff's conduct was so unreasonable as to amount to a *novus actus*. In *Sayers* v. *Harlow U.D.C.* (C.A., 1958) a faulty lock on the door of a public lavatory cubicle caused the plaintiff to become trapped inside. She fell and injured herself when the toilet-roll holder onto which she had climbed in order to get out gave way, and damages were reduced under the Law Reform (Contributory Negligence) Act 1945 (see Chap. 5) for the unreasonable manner in which she had attempted her escape.

These two cases illustrate the different approach that may be taken where the damage is caused by a combination of the plaintiff's own act and the defendant's breach. Whether the issue is seen as one of *novus actus* or of contributory negligence (which is the more common approach) will depend upon the nature and quality of the plaintiff's conduct, and it may be that a positive act is more likely to break the causal chain than a mere omission (*cf. Knightley* v. *Johns* (C.A., 1982); see below). On any view of the matter *McKew* seems to be a harsh decision. There may be instances where even a deliberate act by the plaintiff will not relieve the defendant of responsibility. Thus, in *Pigney* v. *Pointer's Transport Services Ltd.* (H.C., 1957) the defendants were held liable to a plaintiff whose husband committed suicide as a result of mental depression brought on by an injury caused by the defendants' negligence. In a case such as this it would surely make little sense to stigmatise as unreasonable the conduct of one whose capacity for rational judgment has been impaired by the initial injury. In any event, the decision is presumably justifiable on the basis of the "egg-shell skull" principle. *Meah* v. *McCreamer* is to similar effect, but in *Meah* v. *McCreamer (No. 2)* (H.C., 1986) an action by the plaintiff to recover the compensation awarded to the victims of his assaults failed for policy reasons on the ground that to hold the defendant liable would be to impose upon him an indeterminate liability for an indefinite time. The loss was accordingly held to be too remote.

As far as rescuers are concerned (see Chap. 5), there is generally no question of categorising the plaintiff's conduct as a *novus actus* (*Haynes* v. *Harwood* (C.A., 1935)), unless the danger has passed, in which case it is arguable that a duty is no longer owed (see *Cutler* v. *United Dairies (London) Ltd.* (C.A., 1933)). It makes no difference whether the rescuer acts on impulse or after conscious reflection (*Haynes* v. *Harwood, per* Greer L.J.).

Intervention of third party

According to Lord Reid in *Dorset Yacht Co. Ltd.* v. *Home Office* (H.L., 1970) the intervention of a third party must have been something *very likely* to happen if it is not to be regarded as breaking the chain of causation. However, this *dictum* should be interpreted in the light of its proper context, namely the potential liability of a defendant for the criminal act of another because a less stringent test may be applied in the case of non-wilful intervention by the third party. In *Knightley* v. *Johns* (C.A., 1982) the defendant negligently caused a crash on a dangerous bend in a one-way tunnel. The police inspector at the scene of the accident forgot to close the tunnel to oncoming traffic as he ought to have done in accordance with standing orders, so he ordered the plaintiff officer to ride back on his motorcycle against the flow of traffic in order to do so, and the plaintiff was injured in a further collision. It was said that, in considering whether the intervening act of a third party breaks the chain of causation, the test is whether the damage is reasonably foreseeable in the sense of being a "natural and probable" result of the defendant's breach. A deliberate decision to do a positive act is more likely to break the chain than a mere omission; so too, tortious conduct is more likely to break it than conduct which is not. In this case the inspector's errors amounted to tortious negligence which could scarcely be described as the natural and probable consequence of the original collision, and the defendant was therefore not liable (*cf. Rouse* v. *Squires* (C.A., 1973) where the negligence of a driver

who caused a motorway crash was held to be an operative cause of
the death of X who, whilst assisting at the scene of the accident, was
run down by a lorry negligently driven by the second defendant). A
question which as yet remains unresolved is the extent to which
negligent medical treatment or diagnosis may break the chain of
causation, although the answer will no doubt depend upon the extent
to which the practitioner has departed from the requisite standard of
care. In *Prendergast* v. *Sam & Dee Ltd.* (H.C., 1988) the negligent
misreading by a pharmacist of a doctor's prescription did not relieve
the doctor of his duty to write in a reasonably legible hand, and
liability was apportioned between them.

The problems which arise in those cases involving wilful wrongdoing by third parties may be analysed either in terms of duty or of
remoteness. The former analysis is more usual where the only
damage suffered is that caused by the intervening actor (*e.g.* the
Dorset Yacht case), and if a duty to prevent such damage is held to
exist, it follows that, assuming a breach of the duty, the damage
cannot be too remote (see Chap. 2 for a fuller discussion). Where,
however, the defendant's breach causes some initial damage and
thereby affords an opportunity for further damage to be done by the
third party, the courts tend to view the issue as one of remoteness.
Thus, in *Lamb* v. *Camden London Borough Council* (C.A., 1981) a
local authority whose servants negligently damaged the foundations of
the plaintiff's house was held not liable for subsequent damage done
by squatters who moved in while the house was unoccupied. The
Court of Appeal thought that Lord Reid's observation in the *Dorset
Yacht* case understated the degree of likelihood required, and,
according to Oliver L.J., there may be circumstances where the third
party's act must be virtually inevitable before the defendant can be
held liable (see, *e.g.* *Ward* v. *Cannock Chase District Council* (H.C.,
1986)).

In dealing generally with the question of what amounts to a *novus
actus*, the answer is sometimes to be found by considering whether
the intervening conduct was within the ambit of the risk created by
the defendant's negligence. Thus, an incursion of squatters is not one
of the risks attendant upon undermining the foundations of a building
(*Lamb's* case); but the act of a rescuer who goes to assist another put
in peril by the defendant's negligence clearly is within the risk created
by that negligence and is not therefore a *novus actus* (*Haynes* v.
Harwood (C.A., 1935); see Chap. 5).

Intervening natural force
The defendant will not normally be liable for damage suffered as

the immediate consequence of a natural event which occurs independently of the breach. In *Carslogie Steamship Co. Ltd.* v. *Royal Norwegian Government* (H.L., 1952) the defendants were held not liable for storm damage suffered by a ship during a voyage to a place where repairs to collision damage caused by the defendant's negligence were to be done, even though that voyage would not have been undertaken had the collision not occurred.

It will be apparent from the foregoing discussion that, in the case of intervening acts, foreseeability may be a rough guide in assessing relative degrees of responsibility but it can never be the sole criterion of liability. A number of the cases evince a notable lack of consistency of approach and precision in the use of language, which serves only to mask the policy factors at play in the judicial process.

CHAPTER 5

CONTRIBUTORY NEGLIGENCE AND *VOLENTI NON FIT INJURIA*

CONTRIBUTORY NEGLIGENCE

At common law a plaintiff whose injuries were caused partly by his own negligence could recover nothing. When set up as a defence, the application of contributory negligence does not depend upon any duty owed by the injured party to the party sued. All that need be proved is that the plaintiff "did not in his own interest take reasonable care of himself and contributed, by this want of care, to his own injury" (Lord Simon in *Nance* v. *British Columbia Electric Ry.* (P.C., 1951)). Since the Law Reform (Contributory Negligence) Act 1945, contributory negligence is no longer a complete bar to recovery. Section 1(1) of the Act provides that where a person suffers damage as a result partly of his own fault and partly of the fault of another, his claim shall not be defeated but his damages will be reduced to such extent as the court thinks just and equitable having regard to the claimant's share in the responsibility for the damage.

According to section 4 of the Act "fault" means negligence, breach of statutory duty or other act or omission which gives rise to a liability in tort or would, apart from the Act, give rise to the defence of contributory negligence. The defence is therefore applicable not only to a negligence claim, but to a number of other torts, though it does not apply to intentional interference with goods nor to deceit. In *Forsikringsaktieselskapet Vesta* v. *Butcher* (C.A., 1988) it was held that the Act does not apply to claims in contract where the defendant's liability either does not depend on negligence or arises from a contractual obligation which is expressed in terms of taking care, but which does not correspond to a common law duty to take care which would exist in the given case independently of contract. But it does apply where the defendant's liability in contract is the same as his liability in the tort of negligence independently of the existence of any contract, so that the plaintiff cannot avoid the apportionment provisions of the Act by suing in contract alone.

Causation

The damage suffered must be caused partly by the fault of the plaintiff and it is therefore irrelevant that his fault was nothing to do with the accident. Thus, reductions have been made for failing to wear a seat belt or a crash helmet, and for travelling in a vehicle with a drunk driver. To put the matter another way the plaintiff's damage must be within the risk to which he unreasonably exposed himself. In *Jones* v. *Livox Quarries Ltd.* (C.A., 1952) the plaintiff, contrary to instructions, stood on the rear towbar of a vehicle and was injured when another vehicle ran into the back of it. It was held that this was one of the risks to which he had exposed himself and his damages were reduced accordingly. On the other hand, where an employee fell through a rotten floor in a room housing dangerous machinery which bore a notice forbidding him to enter, no reduction was made because that was not a risk which he could have foreseen (*Westwood* v. *Post Office* (H.L., 1974)). Since the whole doctrine of contributory negligence is part of the broader issue of causation, there is nothing to prevent the court in an extreme case from holding the plaintiff 100 per cent. contributorily negligent (*Jayes* v. *IMI (Kynoch) Ltd.* (C.A., 1985)).

Standard of care

The plaintiff is expected to show an objective standard of reasonable care in much the same way as the defendant must to avoid tortious negligence. He is thus guilty of contributory negligence if he ought reasonably to have foreseen that, if he did not act as a reasonable man, he might be hurt himself. Similar factors to those determining whether the defendant is in breach of duty (see Chap. 3) are therefore relevant here.

Particular cases

1. Children

Children are not, by virtue of their minority, in a privileged position as such, but the degree of care to be expected must be proportioned to the age of the child. In *Gough* v. *Thorne* (C.A., 1966), for example, a 13-year-old girl who was knocked down by a negligent motorist when she stepped past a stationary lorry whose driver had beckoned her to cross, was held not guilty of contributory negligence. In *Yachuk* v. *Oliver Blais Co. Ltd.* (P.C., 1949) a boy of nine was injured when he set fire to petrol which he had obtained from the defendants by falsely stating why he wanted it. His damages were not reduced, on the ground that it was foreseeable that he might meddle with it and he could not be expected to appreciate its dangerous properties. It should be noted, however, that there is no age below which, as a matter of law, it can be said that a child is incapable of contributory negligence.

2. Old or infirm persons

It seems that some latitude may be given to such persons in assessing whether they are guilty of contributory negligence. Thus, an elderly person who is unable to move quickly enough to get out of the path of a motorist who drives close by in the expectation that he is able to do so may not be penalised (*Daly* v. *Liverpool Corp.* (H.C., 1939)).

3. Rescuers

It is not often that a rescuer will be found guilty of contributory negligence, bearing in mind that, in the face of imminent danger, his reaction is usually instinctive. Thus, in *Brandon* v. *Osborne, Garrett & Co. Ltd.* (H.C., 1924) the defendants negligently allowed a sheet of glass to fall from their shop roof and the plaintiff, believing her husband to be in danger, tried to pull him away and injured her leg. It was held that she was not contributorily negligent. A similar principle applies where the plaintiff is injured in trying to extricate himself from a perilous situation in which the defendant's negligence has placed him, even though with hindsight he is shown to have chosen the wrong course of action (*Jones* v. *Boyce* (1816) cf. *Sayers* v. *Harlow U.D.C.* (C.A., 1958)). That a rescuer may be contributorily negligent, however, is illustrated by *Harrison* v. *British Railways Board* (H.C., 1981), although in this case the plaintiff's alleged lack of care did not relate to anything done in the course of the actual rescue but consisted in his failure to reduce the danger by not doing that which, by the terms of his employment, he ought to have done.

4. Workmen

In relation to actions for breach of statutory duty, this issue is dealt with in Chap. 9. It seems clear from *Westwood* v. *Post Office* (H.L., 1974) that the more lenient approach towards workmen is appropriate only where the action is founded upon the employer's breach of statutory duty and not upon ordinary negligence.

5. Car passengers

Froom v. *Butcher* (C.A., 1976) firmly established that failure to wear a seat belt is contributory negligence, provided of course that such failure causes or contributes to the injury. It was suggested that ordinarily there should be a reduction of 25 per cent. in respect of injuries which would have been avoided altogether, and 15 per cent. in respect of those which would have been less severe. Although these figures are guidelines only they should, according to *Capps* v. *Miller* (C.A., 1989), generally be followed. So, too, a motor-cyclist who fails to wear a crash helmet will have his damages reduced (*O'Connell* v. *Jackson* (C.A., 1972)). It is also clear that to ride in a car in the knowledge that the driver is drunk constitutes contributory negligence, even though the passenger himself is so intoxicated as not to appreciate that the driver is unfit to drive (*Owens* v. *Brimmell* (H.C., 1977)).

Identification

By the doctrine of identification, where a master sues in respect of damage caused by the combined negligence of a servant for whom he is vicariously liable and another defendant, his damages will be apportioned according to the extent of the servant's fault. In such a case the master is said to be identified with his servant.

Apportionment

Apportionment is on a just and equitable basis according to the 1945 Act and, in assessing the plaintiff's reduction, the court may take into account both the causative potency of his act and the degree of blameworthiness to be attached to it. There seem to be no hard and fast rules, however, and a good deal of judicial discretion is exercised in the matter. The Court of Appeal has held that no apportionment should be made unless one of the parties is at least 10 per cent. to blame (*Johnson* v. *Tennant Bros. Ltd.* (C.A., 1954)), although the case seems to have been decided on the ground that the defendant's breach was not a cause of the damage (see *Capps* v. *Miller* (C.A., 1989)).

One final point to note is that a defendant who seeks to rely on the defence must plead it (*Fookes* v. *Slaytor* (C.A., 1978)).

VOLENTI NON FIT INJURIA

This maxim embodies the principle that a person who expressly or impliedly agrees with another to run the risk of harm created by that other cannot thereafter sue in respect of damage suffered as a result of the materialisation of that risk. The defence is commonly called consent or voluntary assumption of risk and, if successful, is a complete bar to recovery.

For the defence to apply, the defendant must have committed what would, in the absence of any consent, amount to a tort. The defendant must prove not only that the plaintiff consented to the risk of actual damage, but also that he agreed to waive his right of action in respect of that damage. The application of the defence is most straightforward in the case of intentional torts, as, for instance, where each party to a boxing match consents to being fairly struck by the other. Most of the problems arise in torts of negligence where the infliction of damage is a risk rather than a certainty.

Knowledge of the risk

Mere knowledge of the risk does not amount to consent. It must be found as a fact that the plaintiff freely and voluntarily, with full knowledge of the nature and extent of the risk, impliedly agreed to incur it (*Osborne* v. *L. & N.W. Ry.* (H.C., 1888)). In *Nettleship* v. *Weston* (C.A., 1971) the plaintiff, whilst teaching the defendant to drive, was injured when the defendant negligently crashed the car. The plaintiff had first inquired of his pupil whether she carried passenger insurance, and it was held that *volenti* did not apply. One member of the court, however, thought that it would have been a defence but for the prior conversation about insurance, which clearly showed that the plaintiff had no intention of waiving his legal rights.

Problems have similarly arisen in relation to passengers travelling with drunk drivers. *Dann* v. *Hamilton* (H.C., 1939) was such a case where, although on the facts the defence failed, it was suggested that it might apply in cases of extreme intoxication on the part of the defendant (but see now *Pitts* v. *Hunt* at the end of this Chapter). There is a distinction, however, between voluntarily running a known risk and voluntarily agreeing to relieve the other party of liability and, in view of the court's power to apportion the blame under the

Law Reform (Contributory Negligence) Act 1945, it is likely that cases of this kind will be dealt with on the basis of contributory negligence (*Owens* v. *Brimmell* (H.C., 1977)).

The plaintiff's consent must be freely given for the defence to succeed, so that, for example, a consent obtained by fraud should not be a defence. A person cannot be genuinely willing unless he is in a position to exercise freedom of choice, free from any feeling of constraint. For this reason the defence is generally not available in actions by employees against their employers (see later in this Chapter).

Express consent

Cases in which the plaintiff expressly consents to run the risk are relatively few. A person may be able to contract out of his liability by relying upon an exemption clause, but a contractual relationship is not necessary. It will be seen, for example, that an occupier of premises may be able to exclude the common duty of care owed to his visitors (see Chap. 8). This is not necessarily the same as *volenti*, however, for an exclusion notice may effectively defeat the plaintiff's claim even though he has no knowledge or appreciation of the particular risk (*White* v. *Blackmore* (C.A., 1972)). In any event, the Unfair Contract Terms Act 1977, s.2(1), now renders void any purported exclusion of liability for death or personal injury caused by negligence and, in the case of other loss or damage, section 2(2) states that reliance upon an exclusion will only be allowed if the notice is reasonable. Section 2(3) further provides that a person's agreement to, or awareness of, such a notice is not of itself to be taken as indicating his voluntary acceptance of any risk. These provisions only apply, however, where there is business liability (see Chap. 8).

Implied consent

What is alleged here is that the facts clearly justify the inference that the plaintiff has undertaken the risk. It is important to note that it is not merely consent to the risk of injury that is relevant, but consent to the breach of duty that may produce that risk. The defence has rarely succeeded in negligence cases for the reason that, since the alleged consent usually precedes the defendant's breach, it is difficult to see how the plaintiff can have full knowledge and appreciation of the risk. In *Wooldridge* v. *Sumner* (C.A., 1963) it was suggested that *volenti* can never apply in an ordinary negligence action in the absence of a contract, although this is a very extreme view.

1. Sporting events

A spectator at a sporting event does not generally consent to negligence by the participants, so no question of *volenti* arises. The cases have sometimes been approached on the basis that, in the flurry and excitement of the sport and in doing his best to win, the participant owes a lower duty to the spectator than in other negligence cases. In *Wooldridge* v. *Sumner* (C.A., 1963) this was expressed as a duty not to act with reckless disregard for the spectator's safety. A more satisfactory solution, however, was suggested in *Wilks* v. *Cheltenham Home Guard Motor Cycle & Light Car Club* (C.A., 1971) where it was said that the standard to be applied was that of the reasonable man in all the circumstances, including the fact that the defendant is doing his best to win. As between the participants themselves, the issue recently arose in *Condon* v. *Basi* (C.A., 1985) where it was held that sportsmen owe to each other a duty of care in the Atkinian sense. What was reasonable conduct, however, depended upon the particular circumstances of the case and a reckless and dangerous tackle in a local, amateur football match was held to be negligent.

2. Workmen

Since *Smith* v. *Baker* (H.L., 1891) a plea of *volenti* by an employer in an action by his employee is almost bound to fail, because the unequal nature of their relationship is such that the employee does not exercise complete freedom of will. Where an employer is sued for his own breach of statutory duty the defence is not available, though it may be raised if an action is brought against the employer vicariously. Thus, in *I.C.I. Ltd.* v. *Shatwell* (H.L., 1965) two experienced workers deliberately conspired to ignore statutory safety regulations binding upon them and were injured as a result. When sued vicariously the defendants successfully pleaded *volenti*; the plaintiff had consented to the conduct which caused his injury and had been fully aware of the risks.

3. Medical treatment

A patient is clearly not *volens* to the risk of negligent medical treatment, but the issue here is whether a failure to fully inform the patient of the risks inherent in a particular form of treatment vitiates consent. In *Sidaway* v. *Board of Governors of the Bethlem Royal Hospital and Maudsley Hospital* (H.L., 1985) it was held that it does not. A doctor's duty to inform is part of the ordinary duty of care which he owes to his patients, so that a failure to warn of known risks *may* amount to negligence.

4. Rescuers

If the defendant, by his negligence, endangers the safety of others such that a rescue attempt is reasonably foreseeable, he owes a duty to the rescuer (*Haynes* v. *Harwood* (C.A., 1935)). It makes no difference that the person imperilled is the defendant himself rather than a third party (*Harrison* v. *British Railways Board* (H.C., 1981)), and the duty owed is wholly independent of any duty owed by the defendant to those who are rescued (*Videan* v. *British Transport Commission* (C.A., 1963)). Nor is there any rule of law to prevent a claim by a professional "rescuer," so that a fireman injured whilst fighting a negligently-started fire may recover (*Ogwo* v. *Taylor* (H.L., 1988)). In these situations *volenti* clearly does not apply. In the first place the rescuer acts under moral compulsion and does not therefore exercise freedom of choice, and secondly, since the defendant's negligence precedes the rescue the plaintiff cannot be said to consent to it and may not even be aware of it at the time (*Baker* v. *T.E. Hopkins & Son Ltd.* (C.A., 1959)). In *Chadwick* v. *British Transport Commission* (H.C., 1967) a rescuer who assisted at the scene of a train crash and who suffered nervous shock as a result of what he saw was held entitled to recover, even though he was in no personal danger. These principles apply equally to the rescue of property (*Hyett* v. *Great Western Ry.* (C.A., 1948)) although it is unlikely that a person would be justified in taking the same risks.

Joint criminal venture

If, during the course of a joint criminal venture, the defendant tortiously injures the plaintiff, the latter may fail in a civil action either because of the maxim *ex turpi causa non oritur actio* (no action can be founded on an illegal act) or, possibly, because he will be deemed to have consented to run the risk. The maxim *ex turpi* is based on public policy though, as stated in Chapter 8, it will not defeat a workman in breach of his own statutory duty. The issue arose in *Ashton* v. *Turner* (H.C., 1981), where the plaintiff passenger sued for injuries caused by the defendant's negligence in driving a get-away car from the scene of a burglary in which both had participated. It was held that, as a matter of policy, no duty of care was owed and that, even if it were, the defence of *volenti* applied. In *Pitts* v. *Hunt* (H.C., 1989), however, it was held that section 148(3) of the Road Traffic Act 1972 (now section 149 of the Road Traffic Act 1988) prohibits any restriction on the driver's liability to his passenger as is required to be covered by insurance, so that *volenti* is not available in an action by a passenger against his driver. The application of this rule of policy is hard to define, but relevant factors presumably include the gravity of the offence and the degree of connection between it and the tortious conduct. Thus, it was held to apply in *Pitts* v. *Hunt* to defeat the claim of a pillion passenger against a motor cyclist, in circumstances where the plaintiff had been drinking with the defendant before the accident, knew that he did not hold a licence and was uninsured, and encouraged the defendant to drive in a reckless manner.

CHAPTER 6

LIABILITY FOR DANGEROUS PRODUCTS

Part I of the Consumer Protection Act 1987, which came into force on March 1, 1988 was enacted to give effect to an EC Directive of 1985, requiring the harmonisation of law on product liability throughout the Community. Subject to certain defences, the Act creates a regime of strict liability, although existing common law rights remain unaffected so that if, for some reason, the Act does not apply a plaintiff may still be able to sue in negligence.

STRICT LIABILITY UNDER THE 1987 ACT

Although a successful claim under the Act is not dependent upon proof of negligence, the plaintiff will have to prove that he suffered damage caused wholly or partly by a defect in a product.

Parties to the action and the meaning of "product"

No mention is made in the Act of who may be able to sue, so anyone who suffers damage would appear to be covered, whether a user of the product in question or not. As far as potential defendants are concerned, section 2(2) provides that the following are liable for the damage:

(a)   the producer of the product;

(b)   any person who holds himself out as producer by putting his name or trade mark or other distinguishing mark on the product;

(c)   an importer of the product into a Member State from a place outside the EC in order to supply it to another in the course of his business.

The term "producer" is defined in section 1(2) to mean either the manufacturer, or the person who won or abstracted the product (*e.g.* as in the case of mineral deposits) or, where the product has not been manufactured, won or abstracted but essential characteristics of which are attributable to an industrial or other process having been carried out, the person who carried out that process. Furthermore, by section 2(3), the mere supplier (*e.g.* retailer) is liable if he fails within a reasonable time to comply with the plaintiff's request to identify one or more of the persons to whom section 2(2) (see above) applies, or to identify his own supplier. It is readily apparent from the foregoing that the potential range of defendants under the Act is considerably wider than at common law.

"Product" is defined in section 1(2) as any goods or electricity and, although the definition of "goods" in a later part of the Act is wide enough to cover fixtures in buildings and component parts of the building itself, there is no liability where goods are supplied by virtue of the creation or disposal of an interest in land. Component parts and raw materials also fall within the definition of "product" as distinct from the overall product in which they are comprised. Thus, where X manufactures a product containing a defective component manufactured by Y which causes damage (*e.g.* a car with faulty brakes), both X and Y are jointly and severally liable. However, section 1(3) in effect provides that the mere supplier of a product containing component parts will not, by reason only of that supply, be treated as supplying those components.

It has been noted that, where essential characteristics of a product are attributable to an industrial or other process having been carried out, the processor may be liable as a producer within the meaning of section 1(2). The failure of the legislature to define "essential characteristics" or "industrial or other process" may present difficulties of interpretation, particularly with regard to foodstuffs. The potential problems are highlighted by section 2(4), which provides that no person shall be liable "in respect of any defect in any game or agricultural produce if the only supply of the game or produce by that person to another was at a time when it had not undergone an industrial process." In other words, farmers and other suppliers of agricultural produce (defined in section 1(2) as "any produce of the soil, of stock-farming or of fisheries") will be exempt from liability unless, at the time of their supply of it to another, it can be said to have been through an industrial process. If it has, the processor may then be liable in accordance with section 1(2), and there is nothing in the Act to suggest that the defect need be attributable to that process.

The meaning of "defect"

According to section 3(1) a product is defective if its safety is not such as persons generally are entitled to expect. The "safety" of a product expressly includes safety "with respect to products comprised in that product" (*i.e.* components and raw materials), and a product may be unsafe not only if there is a risk of personal injury but also if it poses a risk of damage to property. In determining what persons generally are entitled to expect, section 3(2) provides that account shall be taken of all the circumstances including the following specific matters:

(a) the way in which and the purposes for which the product has been marketed, its get-up, and warnings and instructions for use accompanying it;

(b) what might reasonably be expected to be done with or in relation to the product;

(c) the time when the product was supplied by its producer to another.

The reference in (a) to the purposes for which the product has been marketed may indicate that a balance has to be struck between known risks associated with a product and the benefits which it seeks to confer. Adopting this interpretation in the case of drugs, for example, a product which produces harmful side-effects is not necessarily defective if its disadvantages are outweighed by the long-term benefits. With regard to (b), a product which is clearly intended for a particular use may not be defective if it causes damage when put to an entirely different use. Similarly, where the defendant reasonably contemplates that something would be done to the product before use (*e.g.* testing), he may argue that there is no defect if that thing is not done (*cf. Kubach* v. *Hollands* (H.C., 1937); *Grant* v. *Australian Knitting Mills Ltd.* (P.C., 1936)). The provision of appropriate warnings and instructions may clearly be relevant here, and there would therefore appear to be some overlap with (a) in this respect. As far as (c) is concerned, it should be noted that it is the time of supply by the producer to another which is relevant, not the time of supply to the consumer. The concluding words of section 3(2) provide that the mere fact that a product supplied after that time is safer than the product in question does not require the inference that there is a defect. This clearly makes allowance for the fact that improved safety standards are constantly being developed, so that what is considered safe, say, in 1987, will not necessarily be so in 1990.

Damage

Section 5(1) defines damage for the purposes of Part I as death or personal injury, or loss of or damage to property (including land). Claims for property damage are, however, limited in several important respects. First, the defendant will not be liable for damage to the defective product itself, nor for damage to any product supplied with a defective component comprised in it (section 5(2)). A parallel may be drawn here with the common law, where such claims are regarded as being concerned essentially with the quality of the product so that, in the absence of a contract, there is generally no liability in tort on the ground that the loss is purely economic (*Muirhead* v. *Industrial Tank Specialities Ltd.* (C.A., 1986); see Chap. 2). Secondly, there is no liability unless, at the time of the damage, the property was "of a description of property ordinarily intended for private use, occupation or consumption" and was intended by the plaintiff for such purposes (section 5(3)). A person who suffers damage to his business property must therefore sue in negligence. Finally, no claim will lie where its value does not exceed £275, excluding interest (section 5(4)).

Defences

Section 4(1), paragraphs (a) to (f), provides for the following defences:

(a) The defect is attributable to compliance either with a domestic enactment or with Community law.

(b) The defendant did not at any time supply the product to another. A broad definition is given to "supply" in a later Part of the Act to include not only the usual types of supply contract, but also gifts.

(c) The defendant supplied the product otherwise than in the course of his business *and* either he does not fall within section 2(2) (*i.e.* he is not a producer, "own-brander" or importer) or he does so only by virtue of things done otherwise than with a view to profit. Thus, for example, the producer of home-made wine who gives a bottle to a friend (or, indeed, who charges simply to cover the costs of his production) will be protected. But makers and suppliers of goods who sell for fund-raising charitable activities are presumably businesses and, in any event, supply with a view to profit, albeit not their own.

(d) The defect did not exist at the relevant time. By section 5(2) the "relevant time" means, in relation to electricity, the time at which it was generated; as far as all other products are concerned it means, in the case of a defendant to whom section 2(2) applies, the time when he supplied the product to another and, in other cases, the time of the last supply by a person who is within the ambit of that section. The object of this defence is to afford protection to a defendant into whose product a defect is introduced subsequent to his supply of it.

(e) The state of scientific and technical knowledge at the relevant time was not such that a producer of products of the same description as the product in question might be expected to have discovered the defect if it had existed in his products while they were under his control. This is the so-called "development risks" or "state of the art" defence which has provoked considerable controversy, not least because it would appear to offer a wider protection than the corresponding provision of the Directive which it seeks to implement. Whereas Article 7 of the Directive would only allow the defence if the state of scientific and technical knowledge was not such as to *enable* the existence of the defect to be discovered, section 4(1)(*e*) of the Act talks in terms of what *might be expected* to have been discovered by a producer of products of the same description as the product in question. The statutory language may thus lead to the inference that the defendant is to be judged by the standards of the hypothetical, reasonable producer of the same, or similar, products, which is tantamount to saying that the defendant will not be liable in the absence of negligence. It must be remembered, however, that the onus is upon the defendant to establish the defence.

"Relevant time" bears the same meaning as in (d) above and will normally be the time of supply of the product by a person to whom section 2(2) applies. On the other hand, the time for considering whether the hypothetical producer might be expected to have discovered the defect is while the product was "under his control," and it is at least arguable that he does not necessarily relinquish control simply by having supplied it to another.

(f) The defect constituted a defect in a product containing the defendant's component part (or raw material) and was wholly attributable to the design of the overall product or to compliance by the defendant with instructions given by the producer of the overall product.

Apart from the above defences, the effect of section 6(4) is to preserve the plaintiff's contributory negligence as a partial defence to a claim against any person under the Act.

Miscellaneous
It has been noted that the plaintiff must prove that the defect caused the damage. What is not clear from the Act, however, is whether this simply means that a factual causal link must be established, or whether, in addition, there is to be an inquiry into the question of foreseeability (see Chap. 4). It is arguable that, since the Act is silent on the matter, the issue of foreseeability is irrelevant; but it should equally be borne in mind that, at common law, problems of cause generally do involve such an inquiry, and it therefore remains to be seen how the courts will interpret the new legislation.

Three final points are worthy of note. First, although the ordinary limitation rules apply to actions under the Act, there is a long-stop period of 10 years from the relevant time (see above), after which no claim may be brought. Thus, for example, where a product manufactured and distributed in 1987 causes damage in 1998, a claim against the manufacturer will lie only in negligence. Secondly, section 7 of the Act prevents the defendant from limiting or excluding his liability, either contractually or otherwise. Thirdly, section 1(1) states that the purpose of Part I of the Act is to give effect to the Directive and that it should be construed accordingly. Any ambiguity in the Act should therefore be resolved, wherever possible, by reference to the Directive and not merely in accordance with traditional canons of construction.

COMMON LAW NEGLIGENCE

Where the Consumer Protection Act does not apply, the plaintiff must rely upon his existing common law remedies. If he acquires defective goods under a sale or similar supply contract his first line of attack is to sue the supplier for breach of implied undertakings relating to quality. Although these contractual obligations are generally imposed only upon those who supply in the course of a business, they are strict and entitle the plaintiff to recover both in respect of goods which simply fail to work or which are less valuable than those contracted for, and where the defect causes personal injury or damage to property. If the plaintiff does not have a contract, however, or indeed where an action against his supplier is not viable (*e.g.* the supplier is in liquidation), he may pursue an action in tort.

The manufacturer's liability

The source of the duty owed by a manufacturer to the ultimate consumer is to be found in the so-called narrow rule in *Donoghue* v. *Stevenson* (H.L., 1932), expressed by Lord Atkin as follows:

> "A manufacturer of products, which he sells in such a form as to show that he intends them to reach the ultimate consumer in the form in which they left him with no reasonable possibility of intermediate examination, and with the knowledge that the absence of reasonable care in the preparation or putting up of the products will result in an injury to the consumer's life or property, owes a duty to the consumer to take that reasonable care."

The term "products" includes not only comestibles, but such diverse items as lifts, hair-dye, motor vehicles and, in *Dutton* v. *Bognor Regis U.D.C.* (C.A., 1972), buildings. The manufacturer's duty extends to the packaging of the product and to any labels, warnings or instructions for use which accompany it (*Vacwell Engineering Co. Ltd.* v. *B.D.H. Chemicals Ltd.* (H.C., 1971)).

Manufacturer and ultimate consumer

The term "manufacturer" has been judicially interpreted to include any person who actively does something to the goods to create the danger, such as assemblers, servicers, repairers, installers and erectors. In *Malfroot* v. *Noxal Ltd.* (H.C., 1935) an assembler was held liable when the side-car which he had negligently fitted to a motor-cycle came adrift and injured the plaintiff. Mere suppliers may also come within the rule, even though they be unaware of the danger and do nothing positive to create it. Thus, in *Andrews* v. *Hopkinson* (H.C., 1957) a second-hand car dealer was liable for failing to check that an 18-year-old car was roadworthy, with the result that the plaintiff was injured in a collision caused by a failure of the steering. Similarly, in *Fisher* v. *Harrods* (H.C., 1966) a retailer was held liable for supplying dangerous goods without first checking upon the reputability of his supplier.

Apart from the end user of the product, an "ultimate consumer" is any person who may foreseeably be affected by it. In *Stennett* v. *Hancock and Peters* (H.C., 1939) the defendant was held liable for negligently fitting a metal flange to the wheel of a lorry, so that it came off while the vehicle was in motion and struck the plaintiff.

Intermediate examination and causation

The normal rules of causation and remoteness apply (see Chap. 4) and, as elsewhere in negligence, difficulties may arise where the negligence of two or more defendants causes indivisible damage. According to Lord Atkin's formulation of the rule, the duty only arises where there is "no reasonable possibility of intermediate examination," which would suggest that there is no duty where such a possibility exists. From a conceptual point of view, however, it is perhaps preferable to deal with the issue of intermediate examination in terms of causation. Thus, failure by an intermediary to make an examination reasonably expected of him may either break the chain of causation (assuming that the examination would, or should, have revealed the defect) or, given that the manufacturer originally created the danger, both manufacturer and intermediary will be liable, as in the Irish case of *Power* v. *Bedford Motor Co.* (1959). What is clear is that, if the intermediary's failure to examine is to be regarded as severing the causal chain, it must at least have been likely that an examination would be made, so that a mere foreseeable possibility of inspection will not suffice (*Griffiths* v. *Arch Engineering Co. Ltd.* (H.C., 1968)). If, of course, the intermediary acquires actual knowledge of the defect and fails to withdraw the product from circulation, the manufacturer will probably escape liability (*Taylor* v. *Rover Co. Ltd.* (H.C., 1966)), just as he will where the intermediary ignores a clear warning to test the product before use (*Kubach* v. *Hollands* (H.C., 1937)).

Apart from anything that the intermediary may do in relation to the product, regard must equally be had to what the consumer himself does. Failure by the plaintiff to conduct an expected examination or, *a fortiori*, continued use of the product after discovery of the defect, may produce one of two consequences, depending upon the degree of fault. Either the chain of causation will be broken (see, *e.g. Farr* v. *Butters Bros.* (C.A., 1932)), or the loss may be apportioned under the Law Reform (Contributory Negligence) Act 1945. The plaintiff will not be barred from recovery, however, where he has no effective choice in assuming a risk created by a defect of which he is aware (*Denny* v. *Supplies and Transport Co. Ltd.* (C.A., 1950)).

Proof of negligence and damage

The burden rests upon the plaintiff as in any other negligence action; however, despite judicial reluctance to allow the application of *res ipsa loquitur* (see Chap. 3), damage caused by a defect in manufacture, as distinct from a defect in design, may easily give rise to an inference of negligence (*Grant* v. *Australian Knitting Mills Ltd.* (P.C., 1936)). On the other hand, if it is equally probable that the defect arose after the manufacturing process and is wholly unconnected with anything that the manufacturer may have done, the plaintiff will fail (*Evans* v. *Triplex Safety Glass Co.* (H.C., 1936)). The defendant will no longer escape liability, however, merely by showing that he had a fool-proof system of manufacture and quality control, because the very fact of the defect may be evidence of negligence in the operation of the system by a servant for whom the defendant is vicariously liable (*Hill* v. *J. Crowe (Cases) Ltd.* (H.C., 1978)). Where the alleged defect is in relation to the design of the product, the plaintiff may face greater difficulty in that the issue of negligence is to be judged in the light of current knowledge which must be proved to have been such as to render the damage foreseeable (*cf.* the "state of the art" defence under section 4(1)(*e*) of the Consumer Protection Act 1987 where it is for the defendant to prove that such knowledge did not exist).

As far as damage is concerned, liability only exists for dangerous products which cause personal injury or damage to other property. In the light of the present status of *Junior Books Ltd.* v. *Veitchi Co. Ltd.* (H.L., 1982), and having regard to *Muirhead* v. *Industrial Tank Specialities Ltd.* (C.A., 1985), the defendant incurs no liability in respect of goods which are simply shoddy, for the loss in this case is purely economic. It is further doubtful whether the cost of repairing defective goods which pose an imminent threat of injury to the person or other property is now recoverable, as once it was (at least where the product in question was a building; see Chap. 2 on Economic Loss).

Chapter 7

EMPLOYER'S LIABILITY AT COMMON LAW

This chapter is concerned with an employer's liability to his employees; the incidence of his vicarious liability to third parties is dealt with in Chapter 14. Since 1948 this country has had a national insurance system providing benefits to the victims of industrial accidents and to those who contract certain prescribed industrial diseases. Although the statutory scheme is not dependent upon proof of fault, it has not led to any diminution in the number of actions brought by employees against their employers. In addition to his common law duty there is a large body of statutory obligations cast upon the employer for the protection of his workmen, and it is not uncommon for an employee to sue both in negligence and for breach of statutory duty (see Chap. 9).

THE NATURE OF THE DUTY

At one time, by the doctrine of common employment, there was an implied term in a contract of service that an employee accepted risks incidental to his employment. One of those risks was that he might be injured by the negligence of a fellow employee for whom the employer was not, therefore, vicariously liable. As means were sought to mitigate the harshness of the doctrine, the concept developed of the personal nature of the duty owed by an employer to his workforce—a duty, in other words, which could not be discharged merely by entrusting its performance to another, no matter how apparently competent that other might be. Although the doctrine was abolished in 1948, the employer's personal duty survives and co-exists with his vicarious liability. Traditionally, the duty is said to be threefold, as explained in the leading case of *Wilsons and Clyde Coal Co. Ltd.* v. *English* (H.L., 1938), namely "the provision of a competent staff of men, adequate material and a proper system and effective supervision." The duty is not absolute but is discharged by the exercise of reasonable care and is thus similar to the duty of care in the tort of negligence generally. It must be emphasised, however, that the employer's obligation is not simply to take care himself, but to see that care is taken by whoever he appoints to act for him. The various aspects of the duty will now be considered.

Competent staff

The abolition of the doctrine of common employment has drastically reduced the significance of this particular aspect of the duty, since an employee will usually be able to sue his employer vicariously for the wrongdoing of a colleague. It remains important, however, where the wrongful act, such as an assault or violent horseplay, takes place outside the course of employment. In this case the employer may be liable for breach of his personal duty if he knew or ought to have known of his employee's vicious or playful tendencies (*Hudson* v. *Ridge Manufacturing Co. Ltd.* (H.C., 1957)). So, too, if an employee is instructed to perform a task for which he has not been properly trained and thereby injures his workmate, the employer may be liable, even though there might be

difficulty in establishing negligence by the employee for the purposes
of vicarious liability.

Safe plant and equipment

The duty here is to take reasonable care to provide proper plant
and equipment and to maintain them as such. This includes the
provision of protective devices and clothing, and, in appropriate
cases, a warning or exhortation from the employer to make use of
such equipment. In *Bux* v. *Slough Metals Ltd.* (C.A., 1973) the
plaintiff foundry worker lost the sight of one eye when splashed with
molten metal. Although the employer had, in compliance with
statutory regulations binding upon him, provided protective goggles,
he was held liable for breach of his common law duty, which
extended to persuading and even insisting upon the use of protective
equipment. This case also demonstrates that compliance with a
statutory obligation, whilst evidence of a discharge of the common
law duty, is not conclusive of the matter.

With regard to injury caused by defective equipment, it was held in
Davie v. *New Merton Board Mills Ltd.* (H.L., 1959) that the duty to
provide proper tools was satisfied by purchase from a reputable
supplier. The decision has now been reversed, however, by the
Employers' Liability (Defective Equipment) Act 1969, which renders
an employer personally liable in negligence if two conditions are met:
first, that the employee is injured in the course of his employment by
a defect in equipment issued by the employer for the purposes of the
employer's business and, secondly, that the defect is attributable
wholly or partly to the fault of a third party (whether identifiable or
not). Strict liability is thus imposed upon the employer if his
employee can prove that some third party, such as the manufacturer,
was at fault, though contributory negligence is a defence. In *Coltman*
v. *Bibby Tankers Ltd.* (H.L., 1988) "equipment" for the purposes of
the Act was widely defined to include a ship.

Safe system of work

This is the expression used to describe such matters as the
organisation of the work, the manner in which it is to be carried out,
the number of men required for a particular task and the part that
each is to play, the taking of safety precautions, and the giving of
special instructions, particularly to inexperienced workers (see *Speed*
v. *Thomas Swift & Co. Ltd.* (C.A., 1943)). Although the duty most
commonly arises where the work is of a routine or repetitive nature,
it also applies where only an isolated act of a particular kind is to be
performed, especially if the operation is of a complicated or unusual

character (*Winter* v. *Cardiff R.D.C.* (H.L., 1950)). The employer does not discharge his duty merely by providing a safe system unless he also takes reasonable steps to see that it is put into operation, and he must be mindful of the fact that workers are often careless of their own safety. On the other hand, it may not be necessary to warn or advise an experienced worker of risks with which he should be familiar.

Safe premises

It is clear that the employer's obligation includes making the premises as safe as the exercise of reasonable care and skill permits, but he is not required to eliminate every foreseeable risk if the burden in so doing is too onerous (*Latimer* v. *A.E.C. Ltd.* (H.L., 1953)). In *Wilson* v. *Tyneside Window Cleaning Co.* (C.A., 1958) it was held that the duty exists equally in relation to premises in the occupation or control of a third party. In appropriate circumstances an employer may therefore be expected to go and inspect the premises to see that they are reasonably safe for the work to be done upon them; but the fact that the employer does not have control of the premises is important in determining whether he has been negligent.

THE SCOPE OF THE DUTY

The duty arises only where the master-servant relationship exists so that it will not, for example, avail an independent contractor. It extends to those acts which are reasonably incidental to the employment and is owed to each employee individually, the consequence of which is that the personal circumstances of the employee must be taken into account, in so far as the employer knew or ought to have known of them. Thus, in *Paris* v. *Stepney B.C.* (H.L., 1951) it was held that, where a garage worker known by his employer to be one-eyed was engaged on work involving a risk of injury to his remaining eye, the employer was under a duty to provide him with goggles. Finally, although the duty is frequently dealt with under its various sub-headings, it is to be remembered that there is in effect but a single duty to take reasonable care in the conduct of operations so as not to subject employees to unnecessary risks.

DELEGATION

Since the duty is personal it is said to be non-delegable, so that the employer does not discharge his obligation by entrusting its performance to another, whether that other be a servant or independent contractor (*Wilsons and Clyde Coal Co. Ltd.* v. *English* (H.L., 1938)). Although, as far as the employment of contractors is concerned, some doubt was cast upon this proposition by *Davie* v. *New Merton Board Mills Ltd.* (H.L., 1959), the widely accepted view is that an employer who entrusts performance of his duty to a person other than a servant remains responsible for the defaults of that person (*McDermid* v. *Nash Dredging & Reclamation Co. Ltd.* (H.L., 1987); see, too, Employers' Liability (Defective Equipment) Act 1969).

CHAPTER 8

OCCUPIER'S LIABILITY

THE OCCUPIERS' LIABILITY ACT 1957

The liability of an occupier in respect of loss or injury suffered by those who come lawfully upon his premises is primarily governed by the 1957 Act. Although it is clear that the duty imposed by the Act arises where damage results from the static condition of the premises, there is some doubt as to whether it applies where the plaintiff is injured in consequence of an activity conducted upon the premises. The balance of authority would suggest that it does, at least where the activity in question is an integral purpose of the occupation, rather than being merely ancillary to it. In any event, since the statutory duty is to take reasonable care, there is little or no difference between an action under the Act and one for breach of the common law duty of care.

Section 2(1) of the Act provides: "An occupier owes the same duty, the 'common duty of care,' to all his visitors, except in so far as he is free to and does extend, restrict, modify or exclude his duty to any visitor or visitors by agreement or otherwise."

The occupier

The Act contains no definition of "occupier" which is simply a term of convenience to denote a person who has a sufficient degree of control over premises to put him under a duty of care towards those who come lawfully on to the premises (*Wheat* v. *Lacon & Co. Ltd.* (H.L., 1966)). Control is thus the decisive factor, and it is immaterial that the occupier has no interest in the land. He may be an owner in occupation, a tenant, a licensee or any person having the right to possession and to permit others to enter the premises. For example, in *AMF International Ltd.* v. *Magnet Bowling Ltd.* (H.C., 1968) building contractors were held to be joint occupiers along with the building owners. But a landlord who lets premises by demise to a tenant is not the occupier thereof for the purposes of the Act, though he remains the occupier of those parts of the premises excluded from the demise, such as an entrance hall or common staircase in a block of flats (*Moloney* v. *Lambeth London B.C.* (H.C., 1966)). Exclusive occupation is not, however, essential, so that there may be more than one occupier of the same premises or part of the premises. The issue of multiple occupation was fully considered in the leading case of *Wheat* v. *Lacon & Co. Ltd.* where the House of Lords held that the residential area of licensed premises was occupied both by the manager who lived there under licence from the brewers, and by the brewers, who could be regarded as occupying either vicariously through their servant (the manager) or because they retained control. It was also made clear that, although two or more people may owe the same common duty of care, the content of their duty might well differ according to the degree of control exercised.

The premises

By section 1(3)(*a*) of the Act, the statutory provisions extend to any fixed or movable structure, including any vessel, vehicle or aircraft. This is apt to include not only structures of a permanent nature but temporary erections such as ladders and scaffolding. But with regard to "vessels, vehicles and aircraft" the Act would appear to apply only to the structural state of the premises, so that where injury is caused to a passenger by, say, negligent driving, the appropriate cause of action is negligence at common law.

Visitors

The statutory duty is owed only to visitors who, by section 1(2), are those who would, at common law, have been either invitees or licensees. The common law distinction between these two categories of entrant is thereby abolished and the vital distinction (which remains unaffected by the Act) is as between the visitor and the trespasser. No difficulty arises where the occupier expressly invites or permits another to enter or use his premises, bearing in mind that such invitation or permission may legitimately be limited either to a particular part of the premises or for a specified purpose. It may be alleged, however, that the occupier has impliedly sanctioned the entry, and whether this is so is a question to be decided on the facts of each case. A tradesman, for example, has an implied licence to walk along a garden path to the front door for the purpose of promoting his business with the occupier, unless of course he has been clearly forbidden to do so. For a licence to be inferred there must be evidence that the occupier has permitted entry as opposed to merely tolerated it, for there is no positive obligation to keep the trespasser out. Moreover, repeated trespass of itself confers no licence (*Edwards* v. *Railway Executive* (H.L., 1952)). It must be said that in some cases the courts have been at pains to infer the existence of a licence. Thus, in *Lowery* v. *Walker* (H.L., 1911), members of the public had for many years used the defendant's field as a short cut to the railway station. The defendant had not infrequently prevented them from so doing, but did nothing further until, without warning, he turned a savage horse into the field. The animal attacked and injured the plaintiff, who succeeded in his action on the basis that he was a licensee, not a trespasser. This, and other cases, were decided at a time when trespassers were afforded little or no protection and, in view of subsequent developments (see later in this chapter), it seems likely that the so-called doctrine of the implied licence will, even if it does not fall into disuse, be far less readily applied.

Three further types of entrant must now be considered. First, those who enter premises for any purpose in the exercise of a right conferred by law are, by section 2(6) of the Act, treated as having the occupier's permission to be there for that purpose (whether they in fact have it or not) and are therefore owed the common duty of care. Secondly, section 5(1) provides that where a person enters under the terms of a contract with the occupier there is, in the absence of express provision in the contract, an implied term that the entrant is owed the common duty of care and, according to *Sole* v. *W.J. Hallt Ltd.* (H.C., 1973)), he may frame his claim either in contract or under the 1957 Act. It is further provided by section 3(1) that where a person contracts with the occupier on the basis that a third party is to have access to the premises, the duty owed by the occupier to such third party as his visitor cannot be reduced by the terms of the contract to a level lower than the common duty of care. Conversely, if the contract imposes upon the occupier any obligation which exceeds the requirements of the statutory duty, then the third party is entitled to the benefit of that additional obligation. Thirdly, those who use public (*Greenhalgh* v. *British Railways Board* (C.A.,

1969)) or private (*Holden* v. *White* (C.A., 1982)) rights of way are not visitors for the purposes of the 1957 Act, though the user of a private right of way is now owed a duty under the Occupiers' Liability Act 1984 (see later in this chapter).

Exclusion of the duty

It has already been seen that the duty owed to a contractual entrant is governed by the terms of the contract and that a person who enters under a contract to which he is not a party is owed, as a minimum, the common duty of care. In the case of non-contractual entrants it is clear that, at common law, an occupier may be able to exclude or limit his liability by notice, provided that reasonable steps are taken to bring it to the visitor's attention and that, upon its proper construction, it is clear and unambiguous. Such was the decision in *Ashdown* v. *Samuel Williams & Sons* (C.A., 1956), where it was held that the plaintiff, who was injured by the negligent shunting of a railway wagon upon the defendant's premises, was defeated in her claim by exclusion notices erected by the defendant stating that persons entered at their own risk and that no liability would be accepted for injury or damage, whether caused by negligence or otherwise.

Despite the criticisms of *Ashdown's* case, section 2(1) of the 1957 Act clearly envisages the possibility of an exclusion of the duty and the decision was followed by a majority in *White* v. *Blackmore* (C.A., 1972). The principle is said to rest upon the basis that if an occupier can prevent people from entering his premises, then he can equally impose conditions, subject to which entry is permitted. It will almost certainly not therefore apply either where the visitor enters in the exercise of a right conferred by law, or where he has, in practical terms, no real freedom of choice (as, for example, where an employee enters the premises in the ordinary course of his employment: *Burnett* v. *British Waterways Board* (C.A., 1973)). Furthermore, some writers have argued that the *Ashdown* principle no longer applies in its full rigour on the ground that, if the duty owed to a trespasser (see later in this chapter) represents a minimum standard below which the occupier cannot go, then that duty must also be owed to all entrants; for to suggest otherwise would be to accord to the trespasser a protection denied to the lawful visitor.

Whatever the present common law position may be, the power of the occupier to exclude or restrict his liability for negligence has been severely reduced by the Unfair Contract Terms Act 1977. Section 2 of the Act provides that a person cannot, by reference to a contract term or to a notice, exclude or restrict his liability for death or personal injury caused by negligence; and, in the case of other loss or damage, he cannot exclude or restrict his liability for negligence unless the term or notice satisfies the requirement of reasonableness. By section 1(1) negligence includes a breach of the common duty of care imposed by the 1957 Act and it matters not whether liability arises directly or vicariously. More importantly, the operation of section 2 of the 1977 Act is confined to those situations where there is "business liability" which is defined in section 1(3) as liability for breach of duty arising from things done in the course of a business or from the occupation of premises used for the business purposes of the occupier. There is no exhaustive definition of "business" though section 14 provides that it includes a profession and the activities of any government department or local or public authority. It should also be noted that section 1(3) has been modified by section 2 of the Occupiers' Liability Act 1984 which enables a business occupier to exclude liability to those whom he allows on to his land for recreational or educational purposes, provided that it is not part of his business to grant access for such purposes.

As a result of these provisions *Ashdown's* case would be decided differently today. But whether *White* v. *Blackmore* (C.A., 1972) is similarly affected is debatable, because in that case private land was used to stage a fund-raising event for charity, and it is not certain whether that would be classed as a business occupation.

The common duty of care

The common duty of care is defined in section 2(2) as "a duty to take such care as in all circumstances of the case is reasonable to see that the visitor will be reasonably safe in using the premises for the purposes for which he is invited or permitted to be there." This is similar to the common law duty of care, and whether the occupier has discharged it depends upon the facts, taking into account such matters as the nature of the danger, the purpose of the visit and the knowledge of the parties. In particular, there is express provision in the Act relating to children, those with special skills, warning notices and independent contractors, and these will now be considered in turn.

1. Children

The Act provides that the amount of care, or of lack of it, which the occupier may expect in the visitor is a relevant consideration, so that, by section 2(3)(a), the occupier must be prepared for children to be less careful than adults. At common law, where a child was injured by some especially attractive but potentially dangerous object

which had allured him on to the land, the occupier could not be
heard to say that the child was a trespasser in relation to the very
thing which had attracted him in the first place. In *Glasgow Corp.*
v. *Taylor* (H.L., 1922), for example, a child of seven died after
eating some poisonous berries which he had picked from a bush in a
public park. The berries had a very tempting appearance to
children, yet the defendant, though aware of their toxic nature, had
neither erected a barrier around the bush nor given any warning. It
was held that there was a good cause of action. If, on the other
hand, there is no dangerous object or allurement upon the land, the
occupier is not liable (*Latham* v. *R. Johnson & Nephew Ltd.* (C.A.,
1913)). Nor is he liable if adequate warning is given to keep away,
or the danger is one which should be obvious even to a child.

In the case of very young children, to whom many ordinarily
harmless things may pose a potential hazard, the courts at one time
applied the doctrine of the conditional licence, a legal fiction
whereby the child was regarded as a trespasser unless accompanied
by a responsible guardian. A different approach was adopted,
however, in *Phipps* v. *Rochester Corp.* (H.C., 1955) in which the
court considered that it was proper to have regard to the habits of
prudent parents who will, where appropriate, either take steps to
satisfy themselves that the place holds no danger for children, or not
permit the child to wander without supervision. This case was
followed in *Simkiss* v. *Rhonnda B.C.* (C.A., 1983) and is clearly
consonant with the provisions of the 1957 Act which state that, in
determining whether the occupier has discharged his duty, regard is
to be had to all the circumstances. One of those circumstances must
be what the occupier is reasonably entitled to expect of a young
child's parents.

2. Special skills

Section 2(3)(*b*) provides that "an occupier may expect that a
person, in the exercise of his calling, will appreciate and guard
against any special risks ordinarily incident to it, so far as the
occupier leaves him free to do so." Thus, in *Roles* v. *Nathan* (C.A.,
1963) the defendant was held not liable for the death of two
chimney sweeps killed by carbon monoxide fumes while sealing up a
flue in the defendant's boiler. Had they suffered injury by falling
through a rotten floorboard the position would, of course, have
been otherwise (*Woollins* v. *British Celanese Ltd.* (C.A., 1966)). In
Salmon v. *Seafarer Restaurants Ltd.* (H.C., 1983) a fireman was
entitled to recover damages when it was reasonably foreseeable that
he would be injured while fighting a blaze caused by the occupier's

negligence, despite the exercise of his special skills (see, also *Ogwo* v. *Taylor* (H.L., 1988)).

3. Warnings

The occupier may, in accordance with section 2(4)(*a*) of the Act, discharge his duty by warning his visitor of the particular danger, provided that the warning is sufficient to enable the visitor to be reasonably safe. Warning notices should be distinguished from exclusion notices. By sufficient warning the occupier discharges his duty, whereas an exclusion purports to take away the right of recovery in respect of a breach. To be effective a warning must sufficiently identify the source of the danger and be brought adequately to the visitor's notice. Mere knowledge of the nature and extent of the risk is not necessarily a bar to recovery, though it may go towards establishing a defence of *volenti non fit injuria* or, more likely, contributory negligence (*Bunker* v. *Charles Brand & Son Ltd.* (H.C., 1969); see Chap. 5).

4. Independent contractors

Where a visitor suffers damage due to faulty construction, maintenance or repair work by an independent contractor employed by the occupier, section 2(4)(*b*) provides that the occupier will not be liable if it was reasonable to entrust the work to a contractor and he took reasonable steps to see that the contractor was competent and had done the work properly. The result of this is that the occupier is not answerable for the defaults of his contractor where he has reasonably entrusted work of a technical nature (such as lift maintenance) to him (*Haseldine* v. *Daw & Son Ltd.* (C.A., 1941)). He will be liable, however, if the work is of such a nature that he could easily have done it himself or checked to see that it had been properly done (*Woodward* v. *Mayor of Hastings* (C.A., 1945)). Where the work is of a particularly complex nature, such as a large-scale construction project, the occupier may reasonably be expected to have the contractor's work supervised by, for example, a qualified architect or surveyor (*AMF International Ltd.* v. *Magnet Bowling Ltd.* (H.C., 1968)). On a point of interpretation it was held in *Ferguson* v. *Welsh* (H.L., 1987) that the word "construction" in section 2(4)(*b*) was wide enough to embrace demolition and that, despite the use of the pluperfect tense in the concluding words of the section, the provision afforded protection to an occupier from liability from dangers created by the contractor's negligence during the course of actually doing the work. The majority also held that where an occupier had notice of an unsafe system of work adopted by the contractor, he could be liable to an employee of the contractor injured thereby, although two of their Lordships thought that any such liability would be *qua* joint tortfeasor rather than occupier.

Damage

By section 1(3)(*b*) of the Act, the statutory provisions apply not only to personal injury but also to damage to property, including the property of those who are not visitors which is nevertheless lawfully on the premises. In *AMF International Ltd.* v. *Magnet Bowling Ltd.* (H.C., 1968) it was held that financial loss cosequential upon damage to property is also recoverable.

Defences

The provisions of the Law Reform (Contributory Negligence) Act 1945 apply and section 2(5) of the 1957 Act provides that an occupier is not liable in respect of risks which the visitor willingly accepts, thus allowing for the defence of *volenti non fit injuria* (see Chap. 5). However, where there is business liability within the meaning of the Unfair Contract Terms Act 1977, section 2(3) of that Act provides that a person's agreement to or awareness of a notice purporting to exclude liability for negligence is not of itself to be taken as indicating his voluntary acceptance of any risk.

THE OCCUPIERS' LIABILITY ACT 1984

Persons to whom the Act applies

The 1984 Act governs the liability of an occupier to "persons other than his visitors" in respect of injury suffered by them on the premises due to the state of the premises or to things done or omitted to be done upon them. The terms "occupier" and "premises" have the same meanings as for the purposes of the Occupiers' Liability Act 1957. The expression "persons other than his visitors" includes trespassers and persons exercising private rights of way, but those using public rights of way are specifically excluded.

The scope of the duty

Section 1(3) of the 1984 Act provides that the occupier owes a duty if:

(a) he is aware of the danger or has reasonable grounds to believe that it exists;

(b) he knows or has reasonable grounds to believe that the non-visitor is in the vicinity of the danger concerned or that he may come into the vicinity of the danger; and

(c)   the risk is one against which, in all the circumstances of the case, he may reasonably be expected to offer the non-visitor some protection.

Whilst paragraph (c) clearly adopts an objective test, it would appear that paragraphs (a) and (b) import a subjective element in that the existence of the duty depends upon the occupier's actual knowledge of facts which should lead him to conclude that a danger exists or that the non-visitor is in the vicinity. If the occupier is not aware of those facts he may not owe a duty, even though a reasonable occupier would have known of them. Such an interpretation is not far removed from the old common law duty of "common humanity" which took into account, along with the occupier's skill and resources, his actual knowledge of the trespasser's presence or of the likelihood of it (*British Railways Board* v. *Herrington* (H.L., 1972)). Although it seems, from the objective wording of paragraph (c), that the individual occupier's skill and resources no longer come into the equation, the position is not entirely clear as regards what knowledge is required. It remains to be seen whether paragraphs (a) and (b) will be interpreted subjectively or objectively.

Where the duty arises section 1(4) states that the duty is to take such care as is reasonable in all the circumstances of the case to see that the non-visitor does not suffer injury on the premises by reason of the danger concerned. This is the usual standard in negligence generally, and whether the occupier has discharged his duty will depend upon the character of the entry, the age of the non-visitor, and the extent of the risk, including the burden that would be imposed upon the occupier in eliminating it.

It is to be noted that the new statutory duty applies only to personal injury or death. Liability for loss of, or damage to, property is expressly excluded by section 1(8).

Defences

Section 1(5) of the Act provides that the occupier may, in appropriate cases, discharge his duty by taking reasonable steps to warn of the danger or to discourage persons from incurring the risk. Whether a warning is effective will depend among other things upon the nature of the risk and the age of the entrant. What is adequate for an adult may not be so for a child, particularly if the danger is an allurement.

The defence of *volenti non fit injuria* is preserved by section 1(6) of the Act. It remains to be seen whether it will be more readily available as against trespassers, though there seems no reason why it should be. In any event the indication in *Titchener* v. *British Railways*

Board (H.L., 1983) is that it will normally be limited to dangers arising from the state of the premises.

Although the Act is silent on the matter, there is nothing to suggest that contributory negligence may not be a defence.

Exclusion notices

There is no mention in the Act of the possibility of excluding liability to the non-visitor, and the provisions of the Unfair Contract Terms Act 1977 do not apply to the 1984 duty. Trespassers pose particular problems because, depending upon the point at which they enter the premises, they may be less likely to see a notice than a lawful visitor. One suggested solution is that the duty under the 1984 Act is a minimum which cannot be excluded so that even the lawful visitor would be protected by it, even though he was aware of an exclusion notice (put up, for example, by a non-business occupier). The objection to this, it has been said, is that it would effectively deprive the occupier of his right to exclude liability entirely as against the lawful visitor, which right was given in the 1957 Act and was left intact, at least for the non-business occupier, by the 1977 Unfair Contract Terms Act.

Liability of non-occupier to trespasser

At common law, the liability of a non-occupier (such as a contractor) to the trespasser rests upon ordinary negligence principles. The fact that the plaintiff is a trespasser in relation to the occupier is not relevant except in so far as the trespasser's presence may be less foreseeable. Thus in *Buckland* v. *Guildford Gas Light and Coke Co.* (H.C., 1949) the defendants, who had erected electricity cables on a farmer's land close to the top of a tree, were held liable to a young girl who climbed the tree and was electrocuted. This decision is unaffected by the 1984 Act, but there are indications in *Herrington's* case that no distinction should be drawn in this respect between occupiers and non-occupiers, in which case the defendants in *Buckland* would now owe the duty of common humanity.

CHAPTER 9

BREACH OF STATUTORY DUTY

Breach by the defendant of an obligation cast upon him by statute (other than one which expressly seeks to impose liability in tort) may, apart from giving rise to any criminal sanction laid down in the Act, also enable a person injured by the breach to bring a civil action for damages for "breach of statutory duty." This is a tort in its own right independent of any other form of tortious liability. Whether a plaintiff can sue depends on whether the statute, upon its proper construction, confers a right of civil action upon him and this is, in theory at least, a question of ascertaining the intention of Parliament.

WAS A RIGHT OF ACTION INTENDED?

As a preliminary step, then, the plaintiff must prove that the legislature intended to create a right to sue. In a few instances Parliament has expressly made known its intention, but in the majority of cases the statute is silent on the issue. It is then for the courts to interpret the enactment in order to discover what that intention is and, to this end, certain guidelines have been established. It should be said at the outset, however, that there is considerable inconsistency in judicial approach to the problem.

If the statute creates a duty but imposes no sanction at all, there is a presumption that a civil action will lie (*Cutler* v. *Wandsworth Stadium Ltd.* (H.L., 1949)). On the other hand *Doe* v. *Bridges* (E.C., 1831) is authority for the view that if the Act provides for a criminal sanction, then prima facie that is the only remedy. This broad proposition was reaffirmed in *Lonrho Ltd.* v. *Shell Petroleum Co. Ltd. (No. 2)* (H.L., 1982) by Lord Diplock, who added that there were two exceptions to it. The first is where the duty is imposed for the benefit or protection of a particular class of individuals, and the second is where the statute creates a public right (*i.e.* "a right to be enjoyed by all those of Her Majesty's subjects who wish to avail themselves of it") and a particular member of the public suffers damage over and above that suffered by the public generally. An example of the first exception is to be found in the way that the courts have consistently held that a civil remedy exists for the benefit of employees injured by a breach of industrial safety regulations (and see section 47(2) Health and Safety at Work, etc., Act 1974). By contrast, road users have usually been denied a remedy, though exceptional cases are *Monk* v. *Warbey* (C.A., 1935—vehicle owner permitting an uninsured person to drive) and *London Passenger Transport Board* v. *Upson* (H.L., 1949—failure by driver to give way on a pedestrian crossing). The second exception rarely arises in practice (for an illustration see *Boyce* v. *Paddington B.C.* (H.C., 1903)) but is similar to the more common situation where a plaintiff who suffers special damage as a result of an interference with a common law right may sue in public nuisance (see Chap. 11).

A right of action has sometimes been refused on the grounds that existing common law remedies are adequate (*McCall* v. *Abelesz* (C.A., 1976)), but it is also arguable that the judges are slow to create new rights where none existed before. In *Atkinson* v. *Newcastle Waterworks Co.* (C.A., 1877) the defendants were held not liable for fire damage to the plaintiff's property which might have been prevented had they maintained a sufficient water pressure as required by statute. An influencing factor in the decision was the disproportionate liability which the defendants might otherwise face, which would make them virtual insurers of property in the locality in respect of damage by fire through failure of the water supply.

In conclusion, the answer to the question whether, in any given case, an individual can sue for breach of a statutory duty is, in the absence either of precedent or a clearly stated Parliamentary intention, something of a lottery. As Romer L.J. remarked in *Solomons* v. *R. Gertzenstein Ltd.* (C.A., 1954), no universal rule has yet been formulated which will solve the problem.

THE ELEMENTS OF THE TORT

If the plaintiff can clear the initial hurdle of showing that breach of the particular duty will in principle ground a right of action, he must then prove the following.

Duty owed to the plaintiff

A statute may impose a duty which is owed to persons generally, but where the duty is imposed for the benefit of a limited class of persons, the plaintiff must show that he belongs to that class, and this will depend upon the wording of the Act. In *Hartley* v. *Mayoh & Co.* (C.A., 1954) the widow of a fireman electrocuted while fighting a fire at the defendants' factory had no cause of action for breach of the relevant regulations because they existed for the benefit of "persons employed," and her husband was not such a person. Similarly, a person working for his own private purposes and after normal working hours is not a "person employed or working on the premises" within the meaning of section 14(1) of the Factories Act 1961 and is thus owed no duty in respect of the fencing of dangerous machinery as required by that section (*Napieralski* v. *Curtis (Contractors) Ltd.* (H.C., 1959)). By way of contrast, it was held in *Uddin* v. *Associated Portland Cement Manufacturers Ltd.* (C.A.,

1965) that a person may still claim the protection of section 14(1), notwithstanding that he is not acting within the course of his employment but has left his allotted task to embark on a frolic of his own. This case was approved in *Westwood* v. *Post Office* (H.L., 1974) where it was held that a defective floor in contravention of the Offices, Shops and Railway Premises Act 1963 entitled an employee to sue, even though he was trespassing in that part of the premises in which the accident occurred. Such trespass may, however, be evidence of an unreasonable failure by the plaintiff to take care of his own safety, in which case there will be a reduction for contributory negligence.

Defendant in breach of duty

It is for the plaintiff to prove that the defendant was in breach of his duty, and once again this can only be ascertained by having regard to the precise wording of the Act. For example, the duty in section 14(1) of the Factories Act 1961 that "every dangerous part of any machinery...shall be securely fenced" does not extend to dangers from materials upon which the machine itself is working (*Eaves* v. *Morris Motors Ltd.* (C.A., 1961)). It must also be determined whether the duty is strict or is discharged by taking reasonable care. The fencing provision under section 14(1) is strict to the extent that in *John Summers & Sons Ltd.* v. *Frost* (H.L., 1955) the defendant was held liable when the plaintiff came into contact with a partially exposed grinding wheel, even though to have fenced it completely would have made the machine unusable. On the other hand, it is enacted by section 29(1) of the 1961 Act that a safe means of access to the workplace shall be provided "so far as reasonably practicable" and, according to Denning L.J. in *Levesley* v. *Thomas Firth & John Brown Ltd.* (C.A., 1953) such qualifying words render the duty similar to the common law duty between employers and workmen (see Chap. 7).

Damage of the contemplated type

For the plaintiff to succeed the harm suffered must be of a type which the Act was designed to prevent. In *Gorris* v. *Scott* (Ex., 1874) the plaintiff's sheep were swept overboard the defendant's vessel during a storm. The sheep were not penned contrary to statutory regulations, but the plaintiff nevertheless failed in his action because the object of the regulations was to prevent the spread of disease, not to afford protection from the perils of the sea. So, too, it has been held that the aim of the fencing provisions of the Factories Acts is to prevent the operator from coming into contact with the machine and not to stop parts of the machine, or the materials on which it is working, from flying out and striking the operator (*Close* v. *Steel Co. of Wales* (H.L., 1962)). There has been a tendency in more recent times, however, to adopt a more flexible approach. In *Donaghey* v. *Boulton & Paul Ltd.* (H.L., 1968) the plaintiff slipped and fell through an open space in an asbestos roof on which he was working. In breach of their duty the defendants had failed to provide him with adequate crawling boards, but argued that the expressed object of the regulations was to prevent workers from falling through fragile roofing materials, not through holes in the roof. The House of Lords rejected such a narrow interpretation and held the defendants liable. Lord Reid said that if the damage is of a kind which the regulation seeks to prevent, it matters not that it happens in a manner not contemplated by the enactment.

Causation

The burden rests upon the plaintiff to prove on a balance of probabilities that the breach of statutory duty caused or materially contributed to the damage (*Bonnington Castings Ltd.* v. *Wardlaw* (H.L., 1956)). In this respect there is no distinction between this tort and a common law negligence action, so that the plaintiff must show that he would not have sustained injury but for the defendant's breach. That this may present difficulties where, as is often the case with industrial safety legislation, the breach consists of an omission is illustrated in *McWilliams* v. *Sir William Arrol & Co. Ltd.* (H.L., 1962). An experienced workman fell to his death because he was not wearing a safety harness. Although the employer was in breach of duty for failing to provide a belt he was held not liable since, on the evidence, the deceased would probably not have worn the belt anyway and the accident would still have occurred. At one time it might have been thought that *McGhee* v. *National Coal Board* (H.L., 1973) supported the view that the plaintiff need only establish that the breach materially increased the risk of damage, but it has now been held that that case decided no more than that the plaintiff was entitled to succeed upon proof that the breach materially contributed to the damage (see Chap. 4).

The plaintiff must also show that the damage is not too remote and the usual test of reasonable foresight applies. As in an action for negligence at common law, the precise way in which the damage is caused need not be foreseeable, provided that the other elements of the tort are satisfied (*Millard* v. *Serck Tubes Ltd.* (C.A., 1969)).

On the issue of causation generally, a particular problem arises where it is the plaintiff's own wrongful act which puts the defendant in breach. In *Ginty* v. *Belmont Building Supplies Ltd.* (H.C., 1959) a regulation binding upon both parties required the use of crawling boards on fragile roofs. The defendant had provided the boards and given full instructions as to their use to the plaintiff who, although an experienced workman, neglected to use them and fell through a roof. Both parties were clearly in breach of their statutory obligation but it was held that the plaintiff was the sole author of his injury and his action failed. The *Ginty* principle is in the nature of a defence which was explained by Lord Reid in *Boyle* v. *Kodak Ltd.* (H.L., 1969) in the following terms: "... once the plaintiff has established that there was a breach of an enactment which made the employer absolutely liable, and that that breach caused the accident, he need do no more. But it is then open to the employer to set up a defence that in fact he was not in any way in fault but that the plaintiff employee was alone to blame." Even if the plaintiff is not in breach of his statutory duty he will, for similar reasons, fail in his action if it is his own deliberate act of folly which puts the defendant in breach (*Horne* v. *Lec Refrigeration Ltd.* (H.C., 1965)). The operation of this principle is, however, confined within narrow limits and it will not avail a defendant who is in some way personally at fault. The employer who, for example, fails to provide adequate instructions or supervision or who acquiesces in the breach will still be liable, though there may be a reduction for contributory negligence (see *Boyle* v. *Kodak Ltd.* (above)).

DEFENCES

Volenti non fit injuria

As a matter of public policy this defence is not available to an employer who is sued for a breach of his own statutory duty. In *Imperial Chemical Industries Ltd.* v. *Shatwell* (H.L., 1965) it was held that the defence is available where the plaintiff sues his employer vicariously for the default of a fellow worker, provided that the plaintiff is not of lower rank to, or in the habit of taking orders from, his colleague. In cases other than employer and employee there seems no reason why, in principle, the defence should not be available (see Chap. 5).

Contributory negligence

This is clearly available (see Chap. 5) but, as far as workmen are concerned, the House of Lords in *Caswell* v. *Powell Duffryn Associated Collieries Ltd.* (H.L., 1940) said that regard must be had to the conditions in which they work, bearing in mind the noise, fatigue and repetitive nature of the job. All the same, whilst momentary lapses of concentration may not be too harshly penalised, a finding of contributory negligence is by no means uncommon in this type of case. Indeed, in *Jayes* v. *I.M.I. (Kynoch) Ltd.* (C.A., 1985) the plaintiff was adjudged 100 per cent. contributorily negligent even though the duty was intended, in part, to protect him from his own carelessness; this seems simply to be an alternative way of saying that he was the sole cause of his own injuries. It is to be noted that whilst a breach by the plaintiff of a statutory duty imposed upon him may well amount to contributory negligence, he is not defeated by the principle that a person cannot bring an action arising from his own illegal act (*ex turpi causa non oritur actio*) (*National Coal Board* v. *England* (H.L., 1954)).

Delegation

The general rule is that where a duty is imposed upon a person to perform, he does not discharge it by entrusting its performance to another. Where, however, the alleged delegation is to the plaintiff himself, that is a relevant factor in deciding the issue of causation. In other words it is not so much a question of whether there has been a delegation, but rather whose fault it was that the damage occurred (Pearson J. in *Ginty's* case).

CHAPTER 10

DEFAMATION

Defamation may be defined as the publication of a statement which tends to lower a person in the estimation of right-thinking people generally or which tends to make them shun or avoid him. The latter part of the definition makes it clear that the words need not bring the plaintiff into ridicule or contempt, but may arouse only feelings of pity (*Youssoupoff* v. *M.G.M. Pictures Ltd.* (C.A., 1934)). The aim of the law is to strike a balance between freedom of speech and the right of a man not to have his good name sullied so that, whilst liability is strict in the sense that the defendant's intention is irrelevant, a number of defences are available.

LIBEL AND SLANDER

A defamatory statement or representation in permanent form is a libel, but if conveyed by spoken words or gestures, a slander. Apart from the written word, pictures, statues and waxwork effigies are libels. In addition, radio and television broadcasts are treated as publication in permanent form (Defamation Act 1952) as are words spoken during a theatrical performance (Theatres Act 1968).

Reading out a defamatory document to a third party is, on the balance of authority, a libel (*Forrester* v. *Tyrrell* (C.A., 1893)). To dictate defamatory material to a typist is clearly a slander, but if it is then put into a letter and sent to a third party the dictator publishes a libel through his agent. As far as defamatory matter on records and recorded tapes is concerned, there is a divergence of opinion among writers as to whether this is libel or potential slander.

An important distinction between libel and slander is that libel is actionable *per se*, without proof of special damage, whereas slander requires proof of such, except in the following cases. First, a direct imputation of a criminal offence punishable in the first instance with imprisonment (words conveying mere suspicion of the offence will not suffice). Secondly, an imputation that the plaintiff is presently suffering from a contagious or infectious disease likely to cause others to shun his society. Thirdly, an imputation of unchastity to any woman or girl (Slander of Women Act 1891). Fourthly, words calculated to disparage the plaintiff in any office, profession, calling, trade or business held or carried on by him at the time of the publication. The common law requirement that the words had to be spoken in the way of the plaintiff's calling has been removed by section 2 of the Defamation Act 1952. If, therefore, the natural tendency of the statement is to injure or prejudice the reputation of the plaintiff in his calling the words will be actionable *per se*.

Aside from these exceptions slander requires proof of special damage, which means loss of some temporal or material advantage such as loss of one's job or of the hospitality of one's friends (but mere exclusion from their society is not enough). The damage must not be too remote in accordance with general principles (see Chap. 4), although nervous shock induced by slander not actionable *per se* is considered too remote. Where a third party causes loss to the plaintiff as a result of the statement, that may or may not break the chain of causation depending upon what the defendant ought reasonably to have anticipated. Whilst unauthorised repetition makes the damage too remote, unless there is a legal or moral duty to repeat, the defendant is liable if he intends the repetition or if that is the natural and probable consequence of the original publication (*Cutler* v. *McPhail* (H.C., 1962)).

WHAT THE PLAINTIFF MUST PROVE

Whether the action is for libel or slander the plaintiff must prove that a defamatory statement referring to him was published.

Statement must be defamatory

The words must be defamatory in accordance with the definition already given, though it need not be proved that anyone who actually heard or read them believed them to be true. Where the statement tends to discredit the plaintiff only with a special class of persons, he may not succeed unless people generally would take the same view. In *Byrne* v. *Deane* (C.A., 1937), for example, it was held not to be defamatory to say of a club member that he had informed the police of an illicit gambling machine on the club premises, because right-thinking persons would not think less well of such a man. Problems may arise, however, where the general public is divided in its opinion. Thus, to say of another that he went to work during a strike would certainly lower him in the estimation of a considerable number of people and ought perhaps on that basis to be defamatory. The circumstances in which the statement is made may be important; words spoken at the height of a violent quarrel, for example, are not actionable if those who heard them understood them as mere abuse.

It is a question of law for the judge to decide whether the words are capable of a defamatory meaning and, if they are, it is for the jury to decide whether they are in fact. If the statement is plainly defamatory in its ordinary sense it is actionable (subject to any defence), unless the defendant can successfully explain away the defamatory meaning. Conversely, the words may be prima facie innocent but, in the light of extrinsic facts known to persons to whom the statement is published, bear some secondary defamatory meaning. This is a true, or legal, innuendo and is illustrated in *Tolley* v. *J.S. Fry & Sons Ltd.* (H.L., 1931). The plaintiff, a well-known amateur golfer, was portrayed in an advertisement for the defendants' chocolate. He successfully pleaded an innuendo that he had received payment for his services and had thereby prostituted his amateur status. The extrinsic facts upon which the plaintiff relies in support of the innuendo must be known to the recipients of the statement at the time of publication and the plaintiff must, as a general rule, specify the persons whom he alleges to have knowledge of those facts (*Grappelli* v. *D. Block (Holdings) Ltd.* (C.A., 1981)). It is plain from

Cassidy v. *Daily Mirror Newspapers Ltd.* (C.A., 1929) that it is immaterial that the defendant is unaware of the extrinsic facts.

Where the plaintiff does not rely upon extrinsic facts but merely contends that a particular meaning is to be attributed to the words themselves, there is said to be a "false" innuendo which, unlike the legal innuendo, does not give rise to a separate cause of action. In *Lewis* v. *Daily Telegraph Ltd.* (H.L., 1964) the defendants published a statement that the fraud squad was investigating the plaintiffs' affairs. It was held that those words could not mean, as the plaintiffs alleged, that their affairs were conducted fraudulently, but simply meant that there was a suspicion of fraud, which the defendants admitted was prima facie defamatory but which they could justify.

Reference to the plaintiff

There must be a sufficient indication that the plaintiff is the subject of the statement, and in most cases, at least where the plaintiff is named, this presents no difficulty. The plaintiff need not be named, however, nor need there be any key or pointer in the statement to indicate him in particular, provided that people might reasonably draw the inference that it referred to him (*Morgan* v. *Odhams Press Ltd.* (H.L., 1971)).

It has long been the case that there is no requirement that the defendant must have intended to refer to the plaintiff (*Hulton & Co.* v. *Jones* (H.L., 1910)), and even if the statement is true of one person it may still be defamatory of another. Thus, in *Newstead* v. *London Express Newspaper Ltd.* (C.A., 1940) the defendants were liable for their report that Harold Newstead, a 30-year-old Camberwell man, had been convicted of bigamy, which was true of X but untrue of the plaintiff, who bore the same name, was about the same age, and who also came from Camberwell.

In respect of a defamatory statement directed at a class of persons (*e.g.* doctors) no individual member of that class may usually sue unless there is some indication in the words, or the circumstances of their publication, which indicates a particular plaintiff. But if the reference is to a sufficiently limited class or group (*e.g.* the directors of a company) they may all be able to sue if it can be said that the words refer to each of them individually. These principles were established in *Knuppfer* v. *London Express Newspaper Ltd.* (H.L., 1944).

Publication

There must be publication to at least one person other than the plaintiff or the defendant's spouse, but there is no publication by a typist or printer merely by handing the statement back to its author (*Eglantine Inn Ltd.* v. *Smith* (H.C., 1948)). The defendant is liable if he intends further publication, for example by writing a letter to the correspondence editor of a newspaper (*Cutler* v. *McPhail* (H.C., 1962)). So, too, is he liable if he is negligent, as where he puts a letter in the wrong envelope or speaks too loudly in a crowded room. He is not liable if the statement is overheard by one whose presence is not to be expected, or if a letter is read by one who has no authority to do so (*Huth* v. *Huth* (C.A., 1915)). An unauthorised repetition or republication will break the chain of causation unless the statement is published to one who is under a legal or moral duty to repeat it. The question in each case is whether the defendant ought reasonably to have foreseen that the statement would reach others, though it is probably the case that a high degree of foresight is required.

Every repetition of a defamatory statement is a fresh publication so that, as regards printed matter, the author, editor, printer and publisher are all liable. A mechanical distributor of print, such as a library or newsagent, is presumptively liable but will have a defence if he can prove that he did not know the work contained a libel, and that that lack of knowledge was not due to negligence in the conduct of his business (*Vizetelly* v. *Mudie's Select Library Ltd.* (C.A., 1900)).

A person may be liable for failing to remove defamatory matter placed upon premises by a third party (*Byrne* v. *Deane* (C.A., 1937)). The extent of his duty to do so presumably depends upon whether he has control of the premises where the statement is displayed and the ease with which it can be removed.

DEFENCES

Unintentional defamation

Section 4 of the Defamation Act 1952 provides a defence where the statement is published innocently. The defendant may then make an offer of amends, which means an offer of a suitable correction and apology and, where copies of the statement have been distributed, an offer to take reasonable steps to notify recipients that the words are alleged to be defamatory. If the offer is accepted and duly performed no proceedings may then be taken or continued, but if it is not, the defendant may plead it as a defence provided he published "innocently," and provided he can prove that, if he was not the author, the words were written by the author without malice. Publication is only innocent if either he did not intend to publish the statement about the plaintiff and he did not know of circumstances by virtue of which others might understand it to refer to him; or the statement was not prima facie defamatory and he did not know of circumstances by virtue of which it might be understood to be defamatory of the plaintiff. In either case the defendant must have exercised all reasonable care in relation to the publication, so it is unlikely that the defence, even had it been available at the time, would have succeeded in the *Newstead* case (see above).

Justification

Justification or truth is generally an absolute defence, though the defendant has the onus of proving the truth of the statement. He need only show that the statement is substantially true and whether the defence is lost through a minor inaccuracy is a matter for the jury. Furthermore, section 5 of the Defamation Act 1952 provides that the defence does not fail if the truth of a number of charges cannot be proved, provided that the words not proved to be true do not materially injure the plaintiff's reputation having regard to the truth of the remaining charges. In such a case, the cautious plaintiff will plead only the untrue allegation because the defendant cannot then rely on the publication as a whole and will presumably fail to justify. But, if the plaintiff seeks to adopt this approach, the allegations must be distinct (which is a question of fact and degree) and, if a number of allegations taken together have a common "sting," the defendant is entitled to justify that sting (*Polly Peck (Holdings) plc* v. *Trelford* (C.A., 1986)). If the defendant seeks to justify the repetition of a defamatory statement already made, he must prove that the statement is true, not merely that another made it (*Truth (N.Z.) Ltd.* v. *Holloway* (P.C., 1960)).

Where the defendant's allegation is that the plaintiff has been convicted of an offence, section 13 of the Civil Evidence Act 1968 provides that proof that he stands convicted of it is conclusive evidence that he did commit it. The fact that the plaintiff's conviction is "spent" under the Rehabilitation of Offenders Act 1974 does not prevent the defendant from relying upon justification, but in this case the defence is defeated by proof of malice.

Fair comment

It is a defence that the statement is a fair comment upon a matter of public interest. What is in the public interest is a question of law for the judge and, whilst there is no exhaustive category of such matters, it covers the conduct of government and public institutions, works of art and literature produced for public consumption, theatrical productions and the like. A man's private life is not a matter of public interest unless it reflects upon his ability or fitness for public office.

The comment must be an honest expression of opinion based upon true facts existing at the time the comment was made, though the defence is still available where the comment is based upon an untrue statement made by another on a privileged occasion. If the statement is one of fact rather than opinion the appropriate defence is justification. The facts upon which the comment is based need not be expressly stated but may be impliedly indicated in the circumstances of the publication (*Kemsley* v. *Foot* (H.L., 1952)). As far as the factual basis for the comment is concerned, the defence does not fail merely because the truth of every allegation of fact is not proved, as long as the expression of opinion is fair comment "having regard to such of the facts alleged or referred to in the words complained of as are proved" (Defamation Act 1952, s.6).

The comment mut be fair and the test is whether the defendant was "an honest man expressing his genuine opinion" (Lord Denning M.R. in *Slim* v. *Daily Telegraph Ltd.* (C.A., 1968)), though if the factual basis for the comment is untrue the defence fails, no matter how honest the defendant was. Violent or exaggerated language does not make the comment unfair, but if the plaintiff is charged with base or dishonest motives the defendant must not only show that his opinion was honestly held, but also that there is some foundation for that opinion (*Peter Walker Ltd.* v. *Hodgson* (C.A., 1909)). Comment will not be fair if the defendant is actuated by malice in the sense of evil motive, even though it would have been fair if made by one who genuinely believed it to be true (*Thomas* v. *Bradbury Agnew & Co. Ltd.* (C.A., 1906)). It has been said, although the matter is not settled, that the fact that the author of a letter published in a newspaper is motivated by malice does not prevent the newspaper from setting up the defence (*Lyon* v. *Daily Telegraph Ltd.* (C.A., 1943)). The burden of proving malice rests upon the plaintiff.

Absolute privilege

Statements made on an occasion of absolute privilege are not actionable regardless of whether the defendant was malicious. They include the following:

    (a) Statements made in the course of parliamentary proceedings including reports and papers ordered to be published by either House.

    (b) Statements made during the course of judicial proceedings, whether by judge, jury, counsel or witnesses, provided they are broadly relevant to the issue before the court. The privilege extends not only to proceedings in an ordinary court of law but to any tribunal recognised by law and acting in a similar manner, even though it is not empowered to take a final decision on the issue (*Trapp* v. *Mackie* (H.L., 1979)). This was held in *Addis* v. *Crocker* (H.C., 1961) to include the Disciplinary Committee of the Law Society.

(c) Communications between solicitor and client in connection with litigation. It is not clear whether other communications attract absolute or merely qualified privilege, but in any event what passes between them is only protected in so far as it is reasonably referable to the solicitor-client relationship (*Minter* v. *Priest* (H.L., 1930)).

(d) Communications by one officer of state to another in the course of his official duty (*Chatterton* v. *Secretary of State for India* (C.A., 1895)). It is doubtful whether the privilege extends below communications on a ministerial level, though there may well be a qualified privilege.

(e) Fair and accurate reports in any newspaper (published at intervals not exceeding 26 days) or broadcast from a station, of public judicial proceedings in the United Kingdom (Defamation Act 1952). The report must be published contemporaneously with the proceedings.

(f) Statutory protection is given to various reports of the Parliamentary Commissioner for Administration and of Local Commissioners.

Qualified privilege

This defence exists in respect of statements made for the protection of one's private interests or for the protection of the public interest, as where a complaint is laid before the proper authorities to secure the redress of a public grievance. It is also available where the maker of the statement and the recipient have a common interest in the matter, or where the recipient alone has an interest and the maker is under a legal, moral or social duty to communicate as, for instance, where a reference is given to a prospective employer. The common thread in all of these instances is that the defendant has either an interest or a duty (legal, social or moral) to make the statement. But an equally essential requirement is that the person to whom the statement is made must either have a reciprocal interest or be under a corresponding duty to receive it (*Adam* v. *Ward* (H.L., 1917)).

An illustration of these principles is *Watt* v. *Longsdon* (C.A., 1930). The defendant director of a company received a letter from X, a manager of the company, which was defamatory of the plaintiff, who was managing director. The defendant replied to X in terms defamatory of the plaintiff and he also published X's letter to the company chairman and to the plaintiff's wife. In a libel action against the defendant it was held that his letter to X was privileged because both had a common interest in the company's affairs. The communication of X's letter to the chairman was also privileged on the grounds that the defendant was under a duty to report the matter. However, the defendant was held to be under no duty to communicate the letter to the plaintiff's wife, notwithstanding the obvious interest which she had in receiving it.

Whether or not there is a duty to communicate is a matter of law for the judge and no satisfactory test has evolved. In relation to the press it has been said that there is no defence of "fair information on a matter of public interest" and there is no duty to report that which is based on mere suspicion or conjecture (*Blackshaw* v. *Lord* (C.A., 1984)).

In addition to the above a number of reports are protected, including fair and accurate reports of parliamentary proceedings and of public judicial proceedings. The common law privilege in relation to the latter is wider than the statutory absolute privilege in that it applies to any form of publication made at any time. A number of fair and accurate reports published in newspapers or broadcast from a station in the United Kingdom receive qualified privilege by section 7 of the Defamation Act 1952. The reports so protected are to be found in the Schedule to the Act and are divided into two categories, those in the first being privileged "without explanation or contradiction," and those in the second "subject to explanation or contradiction." The defence is lost as regards those in the second category if the plaintiff requests the defendant to publish a reasonable statement by way of explanation or contradiction and the defendant refuses or neglects to do so.

Qualified privilege may be lost if the defendant publishes the statement more widely than is necessary for the protection of an interest. However, a publication by the defendant to third persons who have no interest or duty is nevertheless protected if it is reasonable and in the ordinary course of business. If, for example, X sends to Y a letter defamatory of Y which he first dictates to his secretary in the ordinary course of business, Y cannot sue for the publication to the secretary provided that the letter is written to protect or further the aims of the business (*Bryanston Finance Ltd.* v. *de Vries* (C.A., 1975)).

The defence is also lost upon proof that the defendant was actuated by malice which may either mean lack of honest belief in the truth of the statement or use of the privilege for an improper purpose. Irrational prejudice or gross or exaggerated language does not amount to malice if the defendant's belief is honest (*Horrocks* v. *Lowe* (H.L., 1975)). His honesty is irrelevant, however, if he makes use of the occasion for an improper purpose as, for instance, where his aim is to spite rather than protect a legitimate interest. Where a defamatory statement is published by an agent on an occasion of privilege, malice on the part of the principal does not affect the agent's protection (*Egger* v. *Viscount Chelmsford* (C.A., 1965)). But if an employee maliciously publishes on a privileged occasion, the employer may be vicariously liable (*Riddick* v. *Thames Board Mills* (C.A., 1977)).

Apology

There are limited circumstances in which an apology may be a defence but in practice the relevant statutory provisions have, for procedural reasons, fallen into disuse. A genuine apology may, however, go in mitigation of damages and its absence may aggravate them.

CHAPTER 11

NUISANCE

For the purposes of an action in tort a nuisance may be either private or public. In addition, there is a large number of statutory provisions aimed at the control of conduct which is damaging to the environment, but these statutory nuisances do not fall within the province of the law of tort since they do not normally give rise to civil liability (but *cf.* Control of Pollution Act 1974).

PRIVATE NUISANCE

The plaintiff may bring an action in private nuisance where the defendant unlawfully interferes with his use or enjoyment of his land or of some right (such as an easement) that he may have in relation to it. What the plaintiff usually complains of is that there has been an "invasion" of his land as a result of some activity which the defendant has conducted upon his own land. Such activity is often not of itself unlawful, but it becomes a nuisance when the consequences of pursuing it extend to the land of his neighbour. Thus, to cause an encroachment upon the plaintiff's land of some tangible thing such as tree roots may be actionable (*Davey* v. *Harrow Corp.* (C.A., 1958)). The distinction between this form of invasion and a trespass is that, in this case, the interference is indirect. Causing physical damage to the land, or to the buildings or vegetation upon it, may constitute a nuisance, as where a drain becomes blocked and floods the plaintiff's land (*Sedleigh-Denfield* v. *O'Callaghan* (H.L., 1940)), or a building is allowed to fall into disrepair with the result that parts of it fall on to the plaintiff's land (*Wringe* v. *Cohen* (C.A., 1940)). In these cases the interference is evidenced by tangible, physical damage, but it may equally be a nuisance merely to interfere with a neighbour's right to have quiet and comfortable enjoyment of his land. This may take a variety of forms, such as creating stench, dust, smoke, noise, vibration and, in *Thompson-Schwab* v. *Costaki* (C.A., 1956) the use of a house in a respectable, residential area for prostitution was held to be actionable (see also *Laws* v. *Florinplace* (H.C., 1981)).

Where the alleged nuisance produces material injury to property, the plaintiff will usually have little difficulty in proving that there has been an unlawful interference with his rights. But if the plaintiff's only complaint is that he cannot enjoy the use of his land to the full, he must prove a substantial interference with the comfort or convenience of living such as would adversely affect the average man. The law must seek to achieve a balance between two competing interests, namely that of the defendant to use his land as he wishes and that of his neighbour not to be seriously inconvenienced by his activities.

Not every interference is actionable, therefore, because people must be expected to tolerate a certain degree of noise or smell in the interests of peaceful co-existence. The interference only becomes unlawful when it is unreasonable.

Unreasonable interference

"The very essence of a private nuisance . . . is the unreasonable use by a man of his land to the detriment of his neighbour" (Lord Denning M.R. in *Miller* v. *Jackson* (C.A., 1977)). The defendant's actual or constructive knowledge of that detriment is a factor in determining whether his conduct is reasonable, but a number of other factors, including the character and duration of the interference, must also be considered. Whether the defendant has unreasonably used his land cannot be gauged solely by reference to the nature of his conduct, because some foreseeable harm may be done which the law does not regard as excessive between neighbours under a principle of "give and take, or live and let live" (*Kennaway* v. *Thompson* (C.A., 1980)). In deciding the issue of reasonable user, the court may have regard to the following matters.

1. Degree of interference

Where physical damage to property has been done, a relatively small interference may amount to a nuisance, but in other cases the interference must be substantial, something more than ordinary everyday inconveniences, such as the plaintiff will be expected to put up with. In *Walter* v. *Selfe* (H.C., 1851) the test was said to be whether there was "an inconvenience materially interfering with the ordinary comfort physically of human existence, not merely according to elegant or dainty modes and habits of living, but according to plain and sober and simple notions among the English people." It is therefore a question of degree as to whether the interference is sufficiently serious, and a good illustration is *Halsey* v. *Esso Petroleum Co. Ltd.* (H.C., 1961) where the defendants were held liable for, *inter alia*, nuisance caused by a nauseating smell emanating from their factory and by the noise at night both from the plant at their depot and from the arrival and departure of petrol tankers.

2. Nature of the locality

A person living in an industrial town cannot expect the same freedom from noise and pollution as one who lives in the country, but this is not a relevant consideration where there is physical injury to property. In *St. Helen's Smelting Co.* v. *Tipping* (H.L., 1865) the defendants were held liable for the emission of fumes from their factory in a manufacturing area which proved injurious to the plaintiff's shrubs.

3. Social utility

The mere fact that the defendant's act is of benefit to the community will not in itself relieve the defendant of liability. Since nuisance is concerned with a balancing of conflicting interests, however, it may be that the plaintiff will have to bear minor disturbances. Once again it is a question of degree and if there is physical damage or the interference is substantial, the public interest should not be allowed to prevail over private rights (*Kennaway* v. *Thompson* (C.A., 1981); *cf. Miller* v. *Jackson* (C.A., 1977)). In *Adams* v. *Ursell* (H.C., 1913) the smell from a fried-fish shop was held to constitute a nuisance to nearby residents, notwithstanding the defendant's argument that he was providing a valuable service to poor people in the neighbourhood.

4. Abnormal sensitivity

A man cannot increase the liabilities of his neighbour by applying his own property to special uses, whether for business or for pleasure (*Eastern and South African Telegraph Co. Ltd.* v. *Cape Town Tramways Co. Ltd.* (P.C., 1902)). Thus, in *Robinson* v. *Kilvert* (C.A, 1889) warm air from the defendant's premises increased the temperature in an upper part of the building and caused damage to stocks of brown paper which the plaintiff stored there. The amount of heat was not such as to cause annoyance or inconvenience to those working for the plaintiff, nor was it harmful to paper generally, so the action failed. The same principle applies to sensitive persons, and no regard is had to the particular needs of individuals such as those with an acute sense of smell or hearing (*Heath* v. *Brighton Corp.* (H.C., 1908)). Once a nuisance is established, however, the plaintiff can recover even in respect of delicate operations, such as the cultivation of orchids (*McKinnon Industries Ltd.* v. *Walker* (P.C., 1951)). It was doubted in *Bridlington Relay Ltd.* v. *Y.E.B.* (H.C., 1965) whether the reception of television signals by a householder was a use of land which the law would protect but this must be regarded as suspect at the present day.

5. State of affairs

It is often said that the interference must be continuous or recurrent rather than merely temporary or occasional. An injunction will not normally be granted unless there is some degree of permanence in the defendant's activities, except in extreme cases (see, *e.g. De Keyser's Royal Hotel Ltd.* v. *Spicer Bros. Ltd.* (H.C., 1914)). Where the plaintiff claims damages the duration of the interference, and the times at which it occurs, are important in determining whether the defendant is liable. A man who builds an extension on to the back of his house no doubt causes inconvenience to his neighbour, but he is not liable for nuisance if he takes all reasonable care to see that no undue annoyance is caused (*Harrison* v. *Southwark and Vauxhall Water Co.* (H.C., 1891)). If, on the other hand, he conducts his operations at unreasonable hours, or takes an inordinately long time, or uses antiquated methods and thereby increases the level of interference, he may be liable (*Andreae* v. *Selfridge & Co. Ltd.* (C.A., 1938)).

An isolated escape is probably not actionable as a nuisance (*S.C.M. (United Kingdom) Ltd.* v. *Whittall & Son Ltd.* (H.C.,

1970)), though it may afford evidence of the existence of a dangerous state of affairs upon the defendant's land. In *Spicer* v. *Smee* (H.C., 1946), for example, defective electrical wiring which started a fire and caused damage to adjacent property was held to constitute a nuisance. Furthermore, there may be liability in negligence or under the rule in *Rylands* v. *Fletcher* (see Chap. 12) in respect of a single escape.

6. Intentional annoyance

If the defendant prosecutes his activity with the express purpose of annoying his neighbour, he will be liable, even though the degree of interference would not constitute a nuisance if done in the ordinary and reasonable use of property (*Christie* v. *Davey* (H.C., 1893)). Thus, in *Hollywood Silver Fox Farm Ltd.* v. *Emmett* (H.C., 1936) the defendant deliberately fired his gun near the boundary of the plaintiff's land in order to disturb the breeding of the plaintiff's silver foxes. Many of the vixens aborted, for which damage the defendant was held liable. An anomalous case is *Bradford Corp.* v. *Pickles* (H.L., 1895) where, in order to induce the plaintiffs to buy his land, the defendant abstracted percolating water, which flowed in undefined channels beneath his land and which fed the plaintiffs' reservoir. His motive was held to be irrelevant and he was therefore not liable. This is distinguishable from *Emmett* on the ground that the plaintiff had no right to receive the water, so that there was no interest to be protected. The right to make noise on one's land, however, is qualified by the right of one's neighbour to the quiet enjoyment of his land. A landowner's right to abstract subterranean water flowing in undefined channels, regardless of the consequences to his neighbour and of his motive, was affirmed in *Stephens* v. *Anglian Water Authority* (C.A., 1987).

Nuisance and negligence

A difficult question is the extent to which negligence is relevant to an action in nuisance. There are numerous dicta to the effect that there are situations where it is not, without further explanation as to what those situations are. If there is a sufficient interference with the plaintiff's rights, it seems that an injunction will be granted regardless of whether the defendant has taken reasonable care because, in deciding whether to grant an injunction, the court is simply concerned with whether the interference is such that the plaintiff ought not to have to tolerate it. Where the claim is for damages, however, fault may be relevant in the sense that the defendant will be liable only if, assuming that the interference is capable of amounting to a nuisance, he knew or should have known that it was likely to occur. It will be seen later in this chapter that there are certain instances in which fault is undoubtedly an essential requirement.

As far as the question of remoteness is concerned, the test is the same in nuisance as in negligence (*The Wagon Mound (No. 2)* (P.C., 1967)).

Damage

In theory damage must usually be proved, either in the form of tangible injury to land or to property upon it, or in the form of substantial inconvenience and discomfort. In some cases the law will presume damage, as where, by the very nature of the interference, it is bound to occur (*Fay* v. *Prentice* (C.P., 1845)). No proof of actual damage is required where the nuisance is to a proprietary right such as an easement.

Although there is no case directly in point, the generally accepted view is that damages for personal injury in private nuisance can be recovered by an occupier. Such injury will usually be consequential upon damage to land or property, or upon interference with the use of the land.

Who can sue

Protection is afforded to those who are in possession or occupation of the land affected. A licensee without possession, such as a hotel guest or a lodger, cannot therefore sue (*Malone* v. *Laskey* (C.A., 1907)). Nor can a landlord out of possession normally bring an action (though of course the tenant can), at least where the interference is with use and enjoyment; but if he can show that permanent damage is likely to be done to his reversionary interest he can sue. An occupier can sue for nuisance even though it was begun before he went into occupation (*Masters* v. *Brent London B.C.* (H.C., 1978)).

Who is liable

1. The creator

The creator of the nuisance is liable whether or not he occupies the land whence the interference emanates (*Hall* v. *Beckenham Corp.* (H.C., 1949)). He remains liable even if he parts with possession and is no longer able to stop the nuisance without committing trespass.

2. The occupier

The occupier will be liable if he creates the nuisance, but, apart from this, he may incur liability either in respect of the acts of others upon his land or where the nuisance existed before he became the occupier. He may, for example, be answerable for those whom he allows on to his land as guests (*Att.-Gen.* v. *Stone* (H.C., 1895)). Although the general rule is that an employer is not liable for the defaults of his contractor, he will be liable if he is under a non-delegable duty, as where there is a withdrawal of support from neighbouring land (*Bower* v. *Peate* (H.C., 1876)), or operations are conducted on or near the highway (*Tarry* v. *Ashton* (H.C., 1876); see Chap. 14). It seems that he will also be liable whenever the work that the contractor is employed to do creates a foreseeable risk of nuisance. In *Matania* v. *National Provincial Bank Ltd.* (C.A., 1936) the occupier of premises who employed contractors to carry out alterations was held liable for nuisance by dust and noise caused to other occupants in the building. In *Spicer* v. *Smee* (H.C., 1946) it was said that "where danger is likely to arise unless the work is properly done, there is a duty to see that it is properly done," but this proposition is probably too wide (*Salsbury* v. *Woodland* (C.A., 1970)).

If a nuisance is created by a trespasser, the occupier is liable not only if he adopts the nuisance for his own purposes (*Page Motors Ltd.* v. *Epsom and Ewell B.C.* (H.C., 1982)) but also if, with actual or constructive knowledge of its existence, he fails to take reasonable steps to abate it (in which case he is said to "continue" the nuisance). This principle was laid down in *Sedleigh-Denfield* v. *O'Callaghan* (H.L., 1940) and has since been extended to dangerous states of affairs which arise naturally upon the land. In *Goldman* v. *Hargrave* (P.C., 1967) a tree on the defendant's land was struck by lightning and caught fire. The defendant had the tree felled and decided to let the fire burn itself out, but it eventually spread to and damaged the plaintiff's land. The defendant was held liable because, with actual knowledge of the danger, he failed to take reasonable steps to abate it (followed in *Leakey* v. *National Trust* (C.A., 1980)); however, it was held in *Home Brewery Co. Ltd.* v. *William Davis & Co. (Leicester) Ltd.* (H.C., 1987) that a lower occupier cannot sue a higher occupier for pemitting the natural flow of water to pass to the lower ground, but that the lower occupier can erect barriers to prevent the flow provided that, in so doing, he does not put his land to an unreasonable use. In this type of case liability is based essentially upon proof of negligence with one important difference, namely that, since the danger is not of the occupier's own making, his individual circumstances should be taken into account, including his financial resources. The test of reasonableness therefore imports a subjective element. As far as the encroachment of tree roots is concerned, liability was imposed without qualification in *Davey* v. *Harrow Corporation* (C.A., 1958). This was approved in *Leakey's* case subject to the proviso that actual or constructive knowledge of the defect was required in accordance with the *Goldman* formula, and it is now clear from *Solloway* v. *Hampshire C.C.* (C.A., 1981) that the defendant is only liable if there was a foreseeable risk of damage by encroachment which he could reasonably be expected to take steps to guard against.

Where a nuisance has been created by the occupier's predecessor the plaintiff must prove that he knew, or ought to have known, of its existence (*St. Anne's Well Brewery Co.* v. *Roberts* (C.A., 1928)).

3. The landlord

Where the premises are let the usual person to sue is the tenant. The landlord will, however, be liable in the following circumstances. First, if he expressly or impliedly authorises the nuisance, as where the interference arises as a result of using the land for the very purpose for which it was let (*Harris* v. *James* (H.C., 1876); *Tetley* v. *Chitty* (H.C., 1986)). In *Smith* v. *Scott* (H.C., 1973) a local authority was held not to have authorised the commission of a nuisance by a "problem" family which it had housed next to the plaintiff. Secondly, he is liable if he either knew or ought to have known of the nuisance before letting the premises. Thirdly, if the premises fall into disrepair during the period of the lease, he is liable if he has reserved the right to enter and repair (*Heap* v. *Ind Coope & Allsopp Ltd.* (C.A., 1940)), and such a right will readily be implied in a short-term tenancy (*Mint* v. *Good* (C.A., 1951); but the significance of this decision is greatly reduced by the Landlord and Tenant Act 1985 which provides that, where a dwelling-house is let for less than seven years, there is an implied covenant by the landlord to keep in repair the structure and exterior of the premises, and certain installations for the supply of essential services). The landlord is clearly liable where he is under an express covenant to repair, but it was held in *Brew Bros. Ltd.* v. *Snax (Ross) Ltd.* (C.A., 1970) that he does not escape responsibility by extracting that obligation from his tenants, provided that he knows or ought to know of the nuisance. In one particular case, that is where premises adjoining a highway collapse and cause injury to a passer-by or to an adjoining owner, liability is, according to *Wringe* v. *Cohen* (C.A., 1940) strict, subject to a defence either that the defect was due to a secret and unobservable process of nature or to the act of a trespasser.

Apart from these common law obligations the landlord may also be liable under the Defective Premises Act 1972, s.4. This provides that if the landlord is under an obligation to his tenant to repair, or has an express or implied power to enter and repair, he owes a duty to take reasonable care to see that all who might reasonably be expected to be affected by defects in the state of the premises are reasonably safe from personal injury or damage to their property.

Defences

1. Prescription

A right to commit a private nuisance may be acquired by 20 years' continuance thereof, provided that the right is capable of existing as an easement. It has been doubted whether the defendant can acquire a prescriptive right to cause unlawful interference by such things as noise, smoke, smell or vibration in which the degree of inconvenience is variable and may at times cease altogether. The plaintiff must have full knowledge of the nuisance before the period begins to run, and there must have been an actionable nuisance during the 20 years. In *Sturges* v. *Bridgman* (C.A., 1879) the plaintiff built a consulting room at the end of his garden and complained of noise from the defendant's premises. The defendant's argument that he had been pursuing his trade for more than 20 years failed, because the interference did not become actionable as a nuisance until the plaintiff extended his premises.

2. Statutory authority

Many nuisance actions arise out of the activitics of bodies authorised by statute to conduct those operations. It is generally a defence to prove that the interference is an inevitable result of what they were obliged or empowered to do, so that there will be no liability without negligence. The following principles were laid down in *Department of Transport* v. *North West Water Authority* (H.L., 1984). First, in fulfilling a statutory duty there is no liability without negligence, whether or not liability for nuisance is expressly preserved in the Act. Secondly, in exercising a statutory power, liability depends upon whether nuisance is expressly preserved; if it is, negligence need not be proved, but if it is not, there is no liability in the absence of negligence (see also Chap. 12).

Precisely what a body is authorised or obliged to do depends upon the provisions of the Act. A liberal interpretation was given in *Allen* v. *Gulf Oil Refining Ltd.* (H.L., 1981) where authority to acquire land and build a refinery was held to confer, by necessary implication, the right to operate the refinery. Since there was no express provision for liability in nuisance, the defendants were held not liable for the inevitable consequences of working the refinery.

3. Coming to nuisance

It is no defence that the plaintiff moved into the area of the nuisance (*Miller* v. *Jackson* (C.A., 1977)).

4. Other defences

Consent and contributory negligence are valid defences, although not likely in nuisance actions. Necessity, act of God, and act of a stranger are defences provided that there is no negligence. It is no defence, however, that the nuisance was the product of the combined acts of two or more persons, though the act of any one individual would not be unlawful (*Lambton* v. *Mellish* (H.C., 1894)).

Remedies

The plaintiff may recover damages for any resulting loss which is of a reasonably foreseeable kind (*The Wagon Mound (No. 2)* (P.C., 1967)).

The remedy of an injunction is an equitable one and will therefore only be granted where damages would be inadequate. If the interference is trivial or temporary it is unlikely to be granted, but it should not be refused simply on the ground that the defendant's activity is in the public interest (*Shelfer* v. *City of London Electric Lighting Co.* (C.A., 1895)). The majority decision in *Miller* v. *Jackson* (C.A., 1977) not to grant an injunction in respect of the frequent escape of cricket balls from the defendant's land because the cricket club was a valuable local amenity, was held to be wrong in *Kennaway* v. *Thompson* (C.A., 1981). An injunction is a flexible remedy and terms may be imposed, for example as to the types of activity permitted and the times at which it may be conducted. This was done in *Kennaway* (above) but the court refused to do so in *Tetley* v. *Chitty* (H.C., 1986), distinguishing *Kennaway* on the ground that, in that case, the defendants had been pursuing their activities before the plaintiff moved into the area.

PUBLIC NUISANCE

A public nuisance may be defined as an unlawful act or omission which materially affects the comfort and convenience of a class of Her Majesty's subjects who come within the sphere of its operation;

whether the number of persons affected is sufficiently large to warrant the epithet "public" is a question of fact (*Att.-Gen.* v. *P.Y.A. Quarries Ltd.* (C.A., 1957)). At common law, public nuisances cover a wide variety of activities such as carrying on an offensive trade, selling food unfit for human consumption and obstructing the highway.

Public and private nuisance

Public nuisance is a crime in respect of which the Attorney-General may, if a criminal prosecution is felt to be inadequate, bring a "relator" action for an injunction to restrain the offending activity.

The same conduct may amount to both a private and a public nuisance, but an individual may only sue in tort in respect of the latter if he has suffered "particular" damage, which means loss or damage over and above that suffered by the rest of the class affected. This encompasses personal injury, and there is clearly no requirement that the plaintiff must have an interest in the land. In *Halsey* v. *Esso Petroleum Co. Ltd.* (H.C., 1961) the plaintiff's washing was damaged by the emission of acid smuts from the defendants' factory, as was the paintwork of his car which was parked in the road outside his house. The damage to the washing was actionable as a private nuisance, whilst that to the car amounted to particular damage for the purposes of an action in public nuisance.

Nuisance on the highway

Perhaps the most common instance of public nuisance is an unlawful obstruction or interference with the public's right of passage along the highway. In *Castle* v. *St. Augustine's Links* (H.C., 1922), for example, the defendant golf club was held liable for so siting one of its fairways that golf balls were frequently sliced on to the highway, with the result that the plaintiff was injured while driving along the road when a ball crashed through the windscreen of his car.

In relation to obstructions, the defendant is liable only if he creates an unreasonable risk, but he is generally liable for the defaults of his contractor because of the non-delegable nature of the duty (see Chap. 14). If the obstruction is reasonable in terms of duration and degree, such as a van delivering goods to a shop, it is generally not actionable.

To conduct one's trade in such a manner as to cause a foreseeable obstruction is actionable, and if such obstruction causes loss of custom to other traders, that is special damage (*Lyons, Sons & Co. v. Gulliver* (C.A., 1914)). But the defendant is not liable for an obstruction, such as a queue outside his shop, which is beyond his control. The plaintiff must in all cases prove damage.

Where damage is done by a projection over the highway, there may be a distinction between artificial and natural things. In the case of the former, liability may be strict (*Tarry* v. *Ashton* (H.C., 1876)), whereas in the case of natural projections (for example, trees) it seems that negligence must be proved and, even though the source of the nuisance is plain to see, the occupier will not be liable until he has actual or constructive knowledge that it is a danger (*British Road Services Ltd.* v. *Slater* (H.C., 1964)). With regard to premises adjoining the highway, the nature of the liability imposed by *Wringe* v. *Cohen* (C.A., 1940) has already been mentioned.

A highway authority is under a duty to maintain the highway and may be liable in negligence, nuisance or for breach of statutory duty under the Highways Act 1980. The Act provides that it shall be a defence to prove that the authority had taken such care as in all the circumstances was reasonably required to make sure that the part of the highway to which the action relates was not dangerous for traffic.

CHAPTER 12

STRICT LIABILITY

THE RULE IN RYLANDS V. FLETCHER

In *Rylands* v. *Fletcher* (H.L., 1868) the defendant employed independent contractors to build a reservoir on his land to supply water for his mill. The contractors discovered some disused mineshafts under the land which, unknown to them, were connected to shafts on the plaintiff's land. They did not seal off the shafts and, when the reservoir was filled, water flowed down them and flooded the plaintiff's mine. Although it was found that the defendant had not been negligent, he was nevertheless held liable for the following reason stated by Blackburn J.: "We think that the true rule of law is, that the person who for his own purposes brings on his lands and collects and keeps there anything likely to do mischief if it escapes must keep it in at his peril, and, if he does not do so, is prima facie answerable for all the damage which is the natural consequence of its escape." In the House of Lords the qualification was added that, in order to be liable, the defendant must have put his land to a non-natural use, and this has since come to be regarded as an essential part of the rule. The main elements of the tort, together with the defences, will now be considered.

Things brought on to the land

In view of the requirement that the defendant must have brought the thing on to his land, it is well established that there is no liability for the escape of things naturally upon the land. Thus, in *Pontardawe R.D.C.* v. *Moore-Gwyn* (H.C., 1929) the plaintiff failed in his action for damage done when an outcrop of rock fell on to his land due to natural erosion. Similarly, the rule was held to be inapplicable to large quantities of thistle seed blown by the wind on to the plaintiff's land (*Giles* v. *Walker* (C.A., 1890)) and to trees, whether planted or self-sown (*Noble* v. *Harrison* (H.C., 1926)). An occupier will, however, be liable if he is instrumental in causing the escape of something naturally upon his land, as where the blasting of explosives caused an escape of rock (*Miles* v. *Forest Rock Granite Co. Ltd.* (C.A., 1918)). He may also be liable in respect of a natural source of danger upon his land if, with knowledge of its existence, he fails to take reasonable steps to abate it, but liability in this type of case is in nuisance or negligence (*Goldman* v. *Hargrave* (P.C., 1967), and see Chap. 11).

The thing must have been brought on to the land for the defendant's own purposes, though this would not appear to mean that he should necessarily derive any personal benefit. In *Smeaton* v. *Ilford Corp.* (H.C., 1954), for example, a local authority under a statutory duty to receive sewage into its sewers was said to come within the scope of the rule. The notion that the defendant is liable only if he collects the thing for his own purposes is closely bound up with the so-called defence of common benefit and recently, in *Dunne* v. *North Western Gas Board* (C.A., 1964), it was doubted whether a public utility under a statutory obligation to collect and supply a substance such as gas could be regarded as accumulating it for its own purposes.

Likely to do mischief

The thing brought on to the land must, if it escapes, be likely to do mischief and this has been equated with "dangerous" things. Many things are capable of doing damage if not properly handled, but if it is the circumstances under which the thing is used rather than the thing itself which produces the danger, the defendant will generally be liable in negligence. "Dangerous" things, on the other hand, are always so because of their intrinsic qualities and, even though the conditions under which they are kept may be adequate to prevent them from doing damage, the danger has not been removed but merely held in check.

The rule of strict liability has thus been applied to a wide variety of "dangerous" things including water stored in bulk, gas, electricity, fire, explosions, vibrations, noxious fumes and poisonous shrubs. In *Hale* v. *Jennings Bros.* (C.A., 1938) liability was imposed for the escape of a fairground roundabout, and in *Shiffman* v. *Order of St. John* (H.C., 1936) a flag-pole which fell and struck the plaintiff was considered, *obiter*, to come within the rule although the defendants in that case were in fact held liable in negligence (it may be wondered whether a flag-pole could properly be regarded as a "dangerous" thing and this, and other, cases lend support to the proposition that the rule is not confined to such things). An extreme illustration is *Att.-Gen.* v. *Corke* (H.C., 1933) where the defendant was held liable for damage done by an encampment of caravan dwellers whom he had allowed upon his land. This decision is questionable, however, especially as liability could equally have been based in nuisance (*Smith* v. *Scott* (H.C., 1973); and see Chap. 11).

Escape

In the absence of an "escape" there is no liability. In *Read* v. *J. Lyons & Co. Ltd.* (H.L., 1947) the plaintiff, whilst working as a munitions inspector, was injured when a shell exploded at the defendants' armaments factory. Although there was an admission that the shell was a "dangerous" thing, it was held that, since there was no allegation of negligence, the defendants were not liable because there had been no escape. There must be "escape from a place where the defendant has occupation or control over land to a place which is outside his occupation or control." An escape caused by a non-natural user is actionable even if the thing which escapes is not the subject-matter of the accumulation (*Miles* v. *Forest Rock Granite Co. Ltd.* (C.A., 1918)). In *Rigby* v. *Chief Constable of Northamptonshire* (H.C., 1985) it was doubted whether the rule applied to the deliberate projection of things on to the plaintiff's land, since trespass is the more appropriate cause of action.

Non-natural user

The defendant must have put his land to a non-natural use which was defined by Lord Moulton in *Rickards* v. *Lothian* (P.C., 1913) in the following terms: "It must be some special use bringing with it increased danger to others, and must not merely be the ordinary use of land or such a use as is proper for the general benefit of the community." What is non-natural is a question of fact and "natural" in this context does not necessarily mean "not artificial," because that which is ordinary and usual, albeit artificial, is not a non-natural user.

The requirement of non-natural user has enabled the courts to adopt a flexible approach and to adapt the application of the rule to changing circumstances of time and place, so that a new situation involving a high element of risk may be brought within the scope of the rule. The modern judicial tendency, however, has been to equate the concept with that of abnormal risk, thus denying the existence of an independent rule of strict liability and assimilating *Rylands* v. *Fletcher* within the general law of negligence. Thus, in *Mason* v. *Levy Auto Parts of England Ltd.* (H.C., 1967) the court, in deciding whether the storage of combustible material amounted to a non-natural user, took account of the quantity of material stored, the manner in which it was stored, and the character of the neighbourhood, and conceded that those considerations might equally have justified a finding of negligence.

It is clear, then, that views of what is non-natural may be modified in the light of changing social conditions. In the past, domestic water supplies, household fires, electric wiring in houses and shops, the ordinary working of mines and minerals and the keeping of trees and shrubs (unless poisonous: *Crowhurst* v. *Amersham Burial Board* (Ex., 1878)) have been held to be natural uses. But the storage of water, gas or electricity in bulk and the collection of sewage by a local authority are non-natural. There are signs, however, of an increasing reluctance by the courts to bring ordinary manufacturing processes within the rule on the ground that they are of general benefit to the community, and the same could be said of the activities of nationalised industries supplying such commodities as gas and electricity. In *British Celanese Ltd.* v. *A.H. Hunt (Capacitors) Ltd.* (H.C., 1969) a factory making electrical goods on an industrial estate was adjudged not to be a non-natural use and in *Read* v. *Lyons* (H.L., 1947) there were dicta to the effect that a munitions factory in time of war was a normal use of land. The requirement of non-natural user is therefore a control mechanism for restricting the range of activities giving rise to liability.

The status of defendant and plaintiff

The rule in *Rylands* v. *Fletcher* is not confined to those who keep or accumulate things on their own land, because the person liable is he who either owns or has control of the thing. Such a person need not necessarily be the owner or occupier of the land but may be a mere licensee (*Rainham Chemical Works* v. *Belvedere Fish Guano Co.* (H.L., 1921)). In *Rigby* v. *Chief Constable of Northamptonshire* (H.C., 1985) it was considered that the rule applied where a dangerous thing was brought on to the highway whence it escaped and caused damage. The occupier of the land from which the thing escapes may also be liable, but only if it is accumulated for his purposes or with his permission.

The plaintiff does not have to be an occupier, but may suffer harm in consequence of an escape on to the land of a third party. In *Charing Cross Electricity Supply Co.* v. *Hydraulic Power Co.* (C.A., 1914) the defendant company, which had statutory authority to carry water beneath the highway, was held liable for flooding from a burst main which damaged the plaintiff's subterranean supply cables.

Damage

The plaintiff can recover for damage to his property and, as was noted in the previous section, he need not be in occupation of land. This is at variance with the view of Lord Macmillan in *Read* v. *Lyons* that the rule "derives from a conception of mutual duties of adjoining or neighbouring landowners," which raises the further problem of whether an action will lie in respect of personal injury. If some of the observations in *Read* v. *Lyons* are correct, the plaintiff must, at least if he is a non-occupier, prove negligence in order to succeed in such a claim, but there is authority to the contrary. For example, in *Shiffman* v. *Order of St. John* (H.C., 1936) the plaintiff succeeded in his claim for injuries received when he was struck by a falling flag-pole which the defendants had erected in a public park. The present position is therefore not free from doubt, although there seems no reason why an occupier cannot recover for personal injury as he was held entitled to do in *Hale* v. *Jennings Bros.* (C.A., 1938) when struck by the defendant's chair-o-plane which came adrift from its moorings and crashed into his stall.

As far as remoteness is concerned the rule itself merely states that the defendant is liable for all damage which is the "natural consequence" of the escape. It is arguable that once it is established that the thing is likely to do mischief if it escapes, it is then immaterial that the escape and resulting damage are not reasonably foreseeable. In this respect an action under *Rylands* v. *Fletcher* may be contrasted with nuisance where an unforeseeable escape is probably not actionable. On the other hand, some writers have suggested that whilst the escape need not be foreseeable, the defendant should only be responsible for those consequences of it which are. The matter has yet to be finally resolved, although in practical terms that which is a natural consequence will in the majority of cases be foreseeable. What is fairly certain is that there can be no claim for pure financial loss because that is damage of a kind for which recovery is restricted (*Cattle* v. *Stockton Waterworks Co.* (H.C., 1875)).

Defences

There are a number of defences, the first three of which mentioned below, together with the concept of non-natural user, have gone a long way towards introducing elements of fault into this area of the law.

1. Act of God

An act of God is an operation of natural forces "which no human foresight can provide against, and of which human prudence is not bound to recognise the possibility." But this is not to say that the defendant will escape liability merely because the event is not reasonably foreseeable. Two cases may be contrasted: in *Nichols* v. *Marsland* (C.A., 1876) the defendant was held not liable when an exceptionally violent rainfall caused his artificial ornamental lakes to flood his neighbour's land. This decision was criticised in *Greenock Corp.* v. *Caledonian Ry.* (H.L., 1917) where, on similar facts, the defendant was held liable on the ground that it is insufficient for him to show that the occurrence was one which could not reasonably be anticipated. He must go further and prove that no human foresight could have recognised the possibility of such an event. For practical purposes the defence is therefore of very limited application.

2. Act of a stranger

The defendant is not liable if the escape is due to the unforeseeable act of a third party over whom he has no control. In *Rickards* v. *Lothian* (P.C., 1913) the occupier of a lavatory was not liable when an unknown person deliberately blocked up the overflow pipe and caused flooding on the plaintiff's premises. The defence is not available, however, if the act is one which the defendant ought reasonably to have foreseen and guarded against. In *Northwestern Utilities Ltd.* v. *London Guarantee and Accident Co.* (P.C., 1936) the defendant's gas main was fractured by a local authority in the course of constructing a sewer. The defendants were held liable in negligence for damage caused by an explosion of the gas because they knew of the work being carried out and, in view of the risks involved, should have checked to make sure that no damage had been done to their mains. In cases such as this a claim based on *Rylands* v. *Fletcher* merges into a claim for negligence, though according to Goddard L.J. in *Hanson* v. *Wearmouth Coal Co.* (C.A., 1939) the onus is upon the defendant to prove both that the escape was caused by the independent act of a third party and that he could not reasonably have anticipated and guarded against it.

For the purposes of this defence a trespasser is a stranger but servants within the course of their employment and independent contractors are not. The defendant is probably responsible for the acts of his family and guests, although the issue is not entirely free from doubt and may depend upon the degree of control which he can be expected to exercise over them. In *Hale* v. *Jennings Bros.* (C.A., 1938) the defendant was held liable for the deliberate act of a lawful visitor in tampering with a potentially dangerous machine.

3. Consent of the plaintiff

Express or implied consent to the presence of the dangerous thing is a defence unless the defendant was negligent (*Att.-Gen.* v. *Cory Bros. & Co. Ltd.* (H.L., 1921)). Consent may be implied where a thing is brought on to the land for the common benefit of the plaintiff and defendant as, for example, where one cistern supplies water to several flats. A further aspect of implied consent is that a person who enters into occupation of property as a tenant takes it as he finds it and cannot later complain about the condition of the premises. In *Peters* v. *Prince of Wales Theatre (Birmingham) Ltd.* (C.A., 1943) the plaintiffs leased a theatre occupied by the defendants and sustained damage to their property when a severe frost caused an escape of water from a sprinkler system in the theatre. The defendants were held not liable in the absence of negligence. In *Northwestern Utilities Ltd.* v. *London Guarantee & Accident Co. Ltd.* (P.C., 1936) the issue of common benefit was held not to be relevant as between the consumer of a product such as gas or electricity, and the statutory undertaker supplying him but dicta in *Dunne* v. *North Western Gas Board* (C.A., 1964) would suggest otherwise.

4. Default of the plaintiff

If the plaintiff's own act or default causes the damage no action will lie. In *Dunn* v. *Birmingham Canal Navigation Co.* (E.C., 1872) the plaintiffs persisted in working their mine beneath the defendant's canal and failed in their action when water flooded the mine. Where the plaintiff is partly at fault the defence of contributory negligence will apply.

If damage is caused only by reason of the extra-sensitive nature of the plaintiff's property he may not, by analogy with nuisance (see Chap. 11), be able to recover (*Eastern and South African Telegraph Co. Ltd.* v. *Cape Town Tramways Co. Ltd.* (P.C., 1902)). However, in *Hoare & Co.* v. *McAlpine* (H.C., 1923) it was thought not to be a good defence that a building damaged by vibrations was exceptionally unstable.

5. Statutory authority

Where there is a mandatory obligation to do a particular thing, the statutory undertaker is not liable for doing that which is expressly required or which is reasonably incidental thereto, unless there is negligence (*Green* v. *Chelsea Waterworks Co.* (C.A., 1894)). This is so regardless of whether liability for nuisance is expressly preserved in the Act (*Department of Transport* v. *North West Water Authority* (H.L., 1983)). Where the statute permits something to be done without a clause imposing liability for nuisance, there is no liability without negligence, but if there is such a clause negligence need not be proved (*Charing Cross Electricity Supply Co.* v. *Hydraulic Power Co.* (C.A., 1914)).

THE ESCAPE OF FIRE

Common law

At common law a person was liable if a fire spread from his premises and did damage to adjoining premises, though there is some doubt as to whether or not liability was strict. He is now liable where the fire is caused by negligence or where it starts or spreads as a result of a non-natural user of land, in which case negligence need not be proved. The latter instance is simply an application of the rule in *Rylands* v. *Fletcher* except that it is not the thing accumulated that escapes, and the test, according to *Mason* v. *Levy Auto Parts of England Ltd.* (H.C., 1967) is whether the defendant brought to his land things likely to catch fire and kept them there in such conditions that if they did ignite the fire would be likely to spread. Although liability under *Rylands* v. *Fletcher* is supposedly strict there seems to be little difference between this formulation and ordinary negligence.

There is a defence in respect of a fire started by an act of God or a stranger, though the defendant may be under a duty to abate a known danger upon his land in accordance with the principle in *Goldman* v. *Hargrave* (P.C., 1967). The term "stranger" applies only to those over whom the defendant has no control, so that there is liability for fires started by the default of a servant (*Musgrove* v.

Pandelis (C.A., 1919)), an independent contractor (*Balfour* v. *Barty-King* (C.A., 1957)), a guest (*Crogate* v. *Morris* (1617)) and perhaps any person lawfully upon his land whom he has authorised or permitted to start a fire (*H. & N. Emanuel* v. *GLC* (C.A., 1971)).

Statute

The Fires Prevention (Metropolis) Act 1774 provides that no action shall lie against a person upon whose land a fire accidentally begins. This provision only applies to fires produced by mere chance or incapable of being traced to any cause. It therefore affords no protection where the fire is caused by negligence or is due to a nuisance or arises from a non-natural user of land. Nor will the defendant escape liability if there is negligence in permitting an accidental fire to spread. In *Musgrove* v. *Pandelis* (C.A., 1919) the defendant was held liable when a fire started in the carburettor of his car in a garage without fault on anyone's part and his chauffeur negligently failed to extinguish it. It was also held that the 1774 Act was no defence to an action brought under *Rylands* v. *Fletcher*. However, if a domestic fire, intentionally lit, spreads without negligence the defendant is not liable (*Sochaki* v. *Sas* (H.C., 1947)). The Act also provided a defence in *Collingwood* v. *Home and Colonial Stores Ltd.* (C.A., 1936) where a fire broke out on the defendants' premises due to faulty electrical wiring but without negligence. In neither of these last two cases could *Rylands* v. *Fletcher* be invoked because there was no non-natural user of land.

CHAPTER 13

LIABILITY FOR ANIMALS

COMMON LAW

A person may incur liability for damage caused by his animals in accordance with ordinary tort principles. Thus the crowing of cockerels may be actionable in nuisance (*Leeman* v. *Montagu* (H.C., 1936)), fox hunters may be liable in trespass if they cause their hounds to enter prohibited land (*League Against Cruel Sports Ltd.* v. *Scott* (H.C., 1985)), and there have been numerous cases in which a person has been held liable in negligence because he owes the ordinary duty to take care that his animal is not put to such a use as is likely to injure his neighbour (Lord Atkin in *Fardon* v. *Harcourt-Rivington* (H.L., 1932)). A modern instance is *Draper* v. *Hodder* (C.A., 1972) where the defendant, whose terriers savaged the infant plaintiff, was held liable for failing to confine them. A defendant is generally not liable if animals naturally upon his land escape and do damage to his neighbour unless he was at fault in permitting their accumulation. Since the decision in *Goldman* v. *Hargrave* (P.C., 1967), however, he may be liable if, with knowledge of a potential threat (albeit not of his making), he fails to take reasonable steps to avert it.

Apart from the above, special rules relating to animals were developed at common law and these were modified by the Animals Act 1971. It should be noted that the Act, with which the remainder of this chapter is concerned, does not affect the availability of common law actions.

STRICT LIABILITY FOR DANGEROUS ANIMALS

The keeper of an animal was strictly liable at common law for damage done by the animal if either it belonged to a dangerous species or it did not so belong but he knew of its vicious characteristics. The 1971 Act preserves the distinction between dangerous and non-dangerous species.

Animals belonging to a dangerous species

By section 2(1) of the Act the keeper of an animal belonging to a dangerous species is liable for any damage caused by it. A dangerous species (which, by s.11, includes sub-species and variety) is one which is not commonly domesticated in the British Islands and whose fully-grown animals normally have such characteristics that they are likely, unless restrained, to cause severe damage or that any damage they may cause is likely to be severe (s.6(2)). With regard to the first part of this definition, the fact that an animal may be commonly domesticated in some other part of the world where it is indigenous, such as a camel, does not affect its classification as a dangerous species (*Tutin* v. *Chipperfield Promotions Ltd.* (H.C., 1980)). Furthermore, once a species has been so classified, the law takes no account of the fact that an individual animal within that species may in truth be harmless, so that the trained circus elephant is treated no differently to the wild elephant in the bush (*Behrens* v. *Bertram Mills Circus* (H.C., 1957)).

As far as the latter part of the definition is concerned, the species envisaged fall into two categories. First, there are those animals which are by natural disposition ferocious and, secondly, those which although normally peaceful have a potential for causing severe damage. There is no definition of "severe" and, by section 11, "damage" includes the death of, or injury to, any person (including any disease and any impairment of physical or mental condition). Since this is not an exhaustive definition the generally accepted view is that "damage" should be given its normal meaning which is wide enough to include damage to property.

Strict liability is thus imposed by section 2(1) but there is no indication in the Act as to what the test for remoteness should be. It has been suggested that, as long as a causal link is established between the animal and the damage, there is no need for the damage to be of a kind normally associated with the animal's characteristics. Support for this view is to be found in *Tutin* v. *Chipperfield Promotions Ltd.* (H.C., 1980) where the defendant was held liable for injuries suffered as a result of a fall from a swaying camel. It would therefore seem that the test is one of direct consequence rather than reasonable foresight.

Animals not belonging to a dangerous species

Strict liability is imposed by section 2(2) for harm done by animals not belonging to a dangerous species. Any animal not coming within the definition of dangerous species in section 6(2) falls into this category. The keeper is liable for damage caused by such an animal if:

(a) the damage is of a kind which the animal, unless restrained, was likely to cause or which, if caused by the animal, was likely to be severe; and

(b) the likelihood of the damage or of its being severe was due to characteristics of the animal which are either abnormal to the species or normal only at particular times or in particular circumstances; and

(c) those characteristics were known to the keeper or to any person in charge of the animal at the time as the keeper's servant or, where that keeper is the head of a household, were known to another keeper who is a member of that household and under the age of 16.

The requirement in paragraph (a) is that the damage must either be of a kind likely to be caused by the animal or of a kind which, if caused, was likely to be severe, in which case it matters not that the damage is not in fact severe. Paragraph (b) presents difficulties in that the animal must either have exhibited abnormal characteristics or normal characteristics given the particular time or circumstances, so the problem is in determining what the normal characteristics of the species are. In *Cummings* v. *Granger* (C.A., 1977) the plaintiff was attacked by an Alsatian dog which the defendant kept to guard his scrap-yard. The Court of Appeal thought it was a normal characteristic of such animals to attack intruders who encroached upon their territory, so that the second limb of paragraph (b) was satisfied. Whether the decision in *Fitzgerald* v. *Cooke Bourne Farms Ltd.* (C.A., 1964) would be the same under the Act is uncertain. The plaintiff in that case failed to recover for injuries caused by the playful antics of a young filly which, in the court's view, was merely indulging its natural instincts. It could now be argued that such characteristics are normal at that particular stage of the animal's development and that the keeper should accordingly be liable.

The keeper must, under paragraph (c), have actual, not constructive, knowledge of his animal's characteristics. But knowledge is imputed to him where he is the head of a household and another keeper under the age of 16, being a member of that household, knew of those characteristics, or where a person in charge of the animal as the keeper's servant knew of them. Finally, as with section 2(1), there is no requirement that the damage be inflicted during the course of an attack or that the animal escape from control (*Wallace* v. *Newton* (H.C., 1982)).

The keeper

Liability under section 2 is imposed upon the keeper who, by section 6(3), is the person who owns the animal or has it in his possession, or is the head of a household of which a member under the age of 16 owns it or has it in his possession. If a person ceases to own or have possession of the animal he will remain the keeper until such time as another person becomes the keeper. Thus, those who abandon unwanted pets do not thereby divest themselves of responsibility. A person who takes possession of an animal to prevent it from causing damage or to return it to its owner does not, merely by so doing, become a keeper.

Defences to liability under section 2

Apart from contributory negligence, which is preserved by section 10, section 5 of the Act contains a number of defences. Thus, there is no liability if the damage is wholly due to the plaintiff's fault (s.5(1)) or he voluntarily assumes the risk thereof (s.5(2)). The first of these defences will apply where, for example, the plaintiff deliberately provokes or teases the animal, or if he goes too close to its cage knowing that it is dangerous (*Marlor* v. *Ball* (C.A., 1900)). As far as the second is concerned, it should be noted that the Unfair Contract Terms Act 1977 does not apply to strict liability under the Animals Act so that a suitably worded notice may be sufficient to exclude liability. An important limitation upon the defence is that, by section 6(5), a keeper's servant is not to be treated as voluntarily accepting risks incidental to his employment. Section 5(3) applies to trespassers and provides that the keeper is not liable for damage done by an animal to persons trespassing upon the premises if either the animal was not kept there to protect persons or property or, if it was kept for that purpose, it was not unreasonable to do so. This does not affect the liability which a person may incur as an occupier under the Occupier's Liability Act 1984 (see Chap. 8). Further, the Guard Dogs Act 1975 makes it a criminal offence to keep a guard dog on business premises (but not on agricultural land or land surrounding a private dwelling) unless either it is secured or under the control of a handler. A keeper who contravenes the 1975 Act is therefore unlikely to be able to claim the protection of section 5(3) since it is doubtful whether he could then be said to be acting reasonably. In *Cummings* v. *Granger* (C.A., 1977) the plaintiff had entered the defendant's scrap-yard as a trespasser knowing that an Alsatian roamed the premises as a guard dog. It was held that, although the damage was not wholly due to the plaintiff's fault, she had nevertheless voluntarily assumed the risk and was also defeated by the defence in section 5(3) (the cause of action arose before the passing of the Guard Dogs Act, so there was no question of the defendant's having committed an offence). No mention is made in the Act of act of a stranger or act of God, so that these are no longer available as defences.

DOGS ATTACKING LIVESTOCK

Section 3 of the Animals Act imposes strict liability upon the keeper of a dog which causes damage by killing or injuring livestock. As well as the more common types of farm animal, "livestock" includes the domestic varieties of geese, ducks, guinea-fowls, pigeons, peacocks and quails, deer not in the wild state, and pheasants, partridges and grouse in captivity. The defences available include those under sections 10, 5(1) and 5(2). In addition, it is a defence under section 5(4) that the livestock was killed or injured on land on to which it had strayed and the dog belonged to the occupier or its presence was authorised by him.

There is a defence in section 9 of the Act to an action for killing or injuring a dog. The defendant must prove that he acted for the protection of livestock and was entitled to do so, and that within 48 hours he notified the police. A person is entitled to act for their protection if either the livestock or the land on which it is belongs to him, or if he is acting under the express or implied authority of such a person. He acts for their protection only if either of the following conditions (satisfied by reasonable belief on his part) applies:

(a) the dog is worrying or is about to worry the livestock and there are no other reasonable means of ending or preventing the worrying; or

(b) the dog has been worrying livestock, has not left the vicinity, is not under anyone's control, and there are no practicable means of ascertaining to whom it belongs.

For the purpose of this section, the Act provides that livestock belongs to a person who owns or has it in his possession and land belongs to the occupier thereof (s.9(5)).

The defence in section 9 applies only to the protection of livestock from marauding dogs, so that if damage is caused to property by other animals (for example homing pigeons eating crops as in *Hamps* v. *Darby* (C.A., 1948)), or if for some reason the statutory provisions are not satisfied, the defendant may fall back on the common law as laid down in *Cresswell* v. *Sirl* (C.A., 1948). This entitles the defendant to take punitive action if the animal is actually attacking his property or there is imminent danger that it will renew an attack already made, and it is reasonable in the circumstances for the protection of that property to kill it.

STRAYING LIVESTOCK

Livestock straying on to another's land

By section 4(1) of the Act where livestock belonging to any person strays on to land owned or occupied by another and causes damage to the land or to property in the ownership or possession of the other person, the person to whom the livestock belongs is liable for the damage. He is also liable for reasonable expenses incurred by the other person in keeping the livestock while it cannot be restored to the person to whom it belongs or while it is detained in pursuance of section 7 (see below), or in ascertaining to whom it belongs. The definition of livestock in section 11 is slightly narrower than for the purposes of sections 3 and 9 since it does not include captive pheasants, partridges or grouse. Livestock belongs to the possessor thereof, so that the owner out of possession, such as a finance company which has bailed the beasts under a hire-purchase agreement, is not liable. There is no liability under this section for personal injuries which means that if such damage is caused the action must be brought either in negligence or, if appropriate, under section 2(2) of the Act.

Defences

The defences laid down in sections 10 and 5(1) apply but, so far as the latter is concerned, section 5(6) provides that damage is not to be treated as due to the fault of the person suffering it by reason only that he could have prevented it by fencing. If, however, any person having an interest in the land is in breach of a duty to fence, the defendant is not liable if the livestock would not have strayed but for that breach. It is plain from the statutory wording that the duty, if such there be, need not be owed by the plaintiff, nor need it be owed to the defendant. A final common law defence is preserved by section 5(5), which states that there is no liability for damage done by livestock which strays from the highway so long as its presence on the highway was lawful. This is not to say that a defendant may not be liable for negligence in such circumstances (*Gayler and Pope Ltd.* v. *B. Davies & Son Ltd.* (H.C., 1924)).

Detention and sale of straying livestock

Under the provisions of section 7 an occupier may detain livestock which has strayed on to his land and which is not under anyone's control. He must notify the police within 48 hours and, if known, the person in possession of the livestock, and he is liable for any damage caused by his failure to treat the animals with reasonable care. The right of detention ceases if the detainer fails to give the requisite notice or is offered an amount sufficient to cover any claim he may have for damage done or expenses incurred under section 4, or if he has no such claim and the possessor of the livestock requests its return. After 14 days' lawful detention the detainer may sell the livestock at a market or by public auction unless legal proceedings have been instituted. Any sum of money realised from the sale in excess of the amount of the seller's claim under section 4 is recoverable by the original possessor of the livestock.

Livestock straying on to the highway

The common law immunity in respect of damage caused by animals straying on to the highway from adjacent land is abolished by section 8(1) of the Animals Act with the result that liability is now determined in accordance with ordinary negligence principles. A landowner is not necessarily obliged to fence his land, and an important factor in deciding whether he has been negligent is the prevailing traffic conditions. In particular, by section 8(2), if he has a right to place his animals on unfenced land he will not be in breach of a duty of care merely by placing them there, so long as the land is in an area where fencing is not customary or is common land or is a town or village green.

CHAPTER 14

VICARIOUS LIABILITY

The general rule is that one who expressly authorises or ratifies a tort is personally liable, but there are circumstances in which a person is liable for the torts of another even in the absence of such authorisation or ratification. The liability which thus arises is known as vicarious liability and the most common example of it is the liability of a master for the torts of his servants committed in the course of their employment.

MASTER AND SERVANT

It is not necessary, for the purposes of the doctrine, that the master be in breach of any duty owed to the injured party (who may himself be either a fellow-servant or a stranger). What is required is that the wrongdoer be a servant and the wrong done in connection with what he is employed to do. The modern justification for the doctrine is that the master is better able to pay because he will insure against such liability, the cost of which is reflected in the price charged for his goods and services. It is also said to act as an inducement to the employer to promote high standards of safety within his organisation.

The meaning of servant

A servant is employed under a contract of service, an independent contractor under a contract for services, but this does not explain the essential distinction between the two types of contract. No single test has yet been devised which is capable of application in all cases, and even the express declaration of the parties as to the nature of their contract is simply one factor to be taken into account (*Ferguson* v.

John Dawson & Partners (Contractors) Ltd. (C.A., 1976)). If the employer controls not only the type of work to be done but also the manner in which it is to be done, that points to a contract of service; but this so-called "control" test has, especially where the task to be performed requires a high degree of skill or expertise, lost much of its use, for the servant will in practice frequently be left to decide for himself how best to carry out the job. In *Stevenson, Jordan and Harrison Ltd.* v. *Macdonald and Evans* (C.A., 1952) Denning L.J. suggested that, under a contract of service, the employee's work is done as an integral part of the business, whereas under a contract for services his work is not integrated into the business but is merely accessory to it. More recently, in *Ready Mixed Concrete (South East) Ltd.* v. *Minister of Pensions and National Insurance* (H.C., 1968) it was held that three conditions must be fulfilled for a contract of service to exist. First, the servant agrees, in consideration of a wage or other remuneration, to provide his own work and skill in the performance of some service for his master; secondly, he agrees to be subject to the other's control to such degree as to make that other the master; thirdly, the other provisions of the contract are consistent with its being a contract of service. A different approach was adopted in *Market Investigations Ltd.* v. *Minister of Social Security* (H.C., 1969) where it was suggested that the basic test is whether the worker is performing the service as a person in business on his own account. In answering this question it is relevant to consider whether the person uses his own premises and equipment, whether he hires his own helpers, the degree of financial risk he takes and the degree of responsibility, if any, which he has for investment and management. Although this approach has been followed in later cases, judicial warnings have been given that the test is not of itself to be regarded as conclusive of the question. All that can be said is that there is no exhaustive category of matters relevant in deciding the issue, and what is regarded as the crucial factor in one case may well be outweighed by different considerations in another.

Lending a servant

A particular problem is that of lending a servant, for the difficulty then arises as to who is the master for the purposes of vicarious liability. In *Mersey Docks and Harbour Board* v. *Coggins and Griffith (Liverpool) Ltd.* (H.L., 1947) the Board hired a crane driver, together with his crane, to X, under a contract which provided that the driver was to be the servant of X. In the course of working the crane the driver negligently injured a third party. Although X had, at the time, the immediate direction and control of what was to be done, they had no power to direct how the crane should be worked. Furthermore, the driver continued to be paid by the Board, which alone had the right to dismiss him. It was held that, notwithstanding the terms of the hire contract, the Board had failed to discharge the heavy burden of proof to shift responsibility for the driver's negligence onto X. This case establishes no universal test but Lord Porter said that factors for consideration are who is paymaster, who can dismiss, how long the alternative service lasts and what machinery is employed. The degree of control exercised by the respective employers is clearly important, and it would seem that the right to control is more readily transferred in the case of an unskilled servant.

The course of employment

For the master to be liable the wrong must be committed in the course of the servant's employment. This will be the case where what the servant does is authorised by the master, or is an unauthorised way of doing that which he is employed to do. Whether or not the act is done in the course of employment is a question of fact, and the modern trend has been to adopt a liberal approach. Thus, a tanker driver who, whilst delivering petrol, lit a cigarette and carelessly discarded a match causing a fire, was held to be acting within the course of his employment. It was said that the act of lighting the cigarette, whilst not in itself connected with his job, could not be looked at in isolation from the surrounding circumstances (*Century Insurance Co. Ltd.* v. *Northern Ireland Road Transport Board* (H.L., 1942)). This case was recently followed in *Harrison* v. *Michelin Tyre Co. Ltd.* (H.C., 1985) where a momentary and dangerous act of horseplay was held, nevertheless, to have been done in the course of employment.

If, on the other hand, the servant's act is wholly unconnected to the job for which he is employed, he is said to be "on a frolic of his own" and the master is not liable. In *Beard* v. *London General Omnibus Co.* (C.A., 1900) the employer of a bus conductor who, in the absence of the driver, negligently drove the bus himself was held not liable. This may be contrasted with *Kay* v. *I.T.W. Ltd.* (C.A., 1968) where the servant attempted to move a lorry belonging to another firm because it was blocking the entrance to his employer's warehouse to which he had been instructed to return a fork-lift truck. It was held that, since the attempted removal of the obstruction was done in order that the servant could complete his own task, the employer was vicariously liable. On the other hand, it was held in *General Engineering Services Ltd.* v. *Kingston and St. Andrew Corp.*

(P.C., 1988) that firemen operating a "go-slow" policy who took five times as long as they normally would have done to drive to the scene of a fire (with the result that the plaintiff's premises were destroyed) were not within the course of employment. The courts have been faced with similar problems where the servant's act has been expressly prohibited. In principle, if the prohibition amounts to a restriction on the class of acts which the servant is employed to do, the master is not liable; but he is liable if the prohibition relates merely to a mode of performing the employment. So a servant who, contrary to written instructions, raced his employer's bus with that of a rival company was held to be within the course of his employment (*Limpus* v. *London General Omnibus Co.* (H.C., 1862)). A number of cases have dealt with the problem of the giving of lifts to unauthorised passengers. It was held in *Twine* v. *Bean's Express Ltd.* (C.A., 1946) that such an act was outside the course of employment, though the view was expressed that, in so far as injury to persons other than the passenger was concerned, the driver would be within the course of his employment. Where a driver's foreman consented to the passenger's presence in the vehicle, however, the master was held liable because the foreman, of whose lack of actual authority the passenger was unaware, was nonetheless acting within the scope of his apparent authority (*Young* v. *Edward Box & Co. Ltd.* (C.A., 1951)). The decision in *Twine's* case is not easy to reconcile with *Rose* v. *Plenty* (C.A., 1976) where a milkman, in allowing a young boy onto his float to help him with his milk round in contravention of his employer's instructions, was held to be within the course of his employment when the boy fell off and was injured. The majority of the court distinguished the earlier case on the ground that the engagement of the boy was done in furtherance of the master's business.

There are cases where the servant's act, although not part of his regular employment as such, is necessarily incidental to it. In *Staton* v. *National Coal Board* (H.C., 1957), for example, a servant cycling to the pay office on his employer's land to collect his pay after work had finished was held to be within the course of his employment. But whilst employment may start as soon as the servant enters his employer's premises, those travelling to or from work are not usually considered to be in the course of employment, unless, of course, they are travelling specifically on the master's business or on some errand which is incidental to it. Thus, a driver who deviates from his route for the purpose of getting a meal may still be within the course of employment (*Harvey* v. *R.G. O'Dell Ltd.* (H.C., 1958); *cf. Hilton* v. *Thomas Burton (Rhodes) Ltd.* (H.C., 1961)). In *Smith* v. *Stages*

(H.L., 1989) a worker travelling between home and a temporary workplace, and who was paid wages during that time, was held to be within the course of employment, notwithstanding that he might have a discretion as to the mode and time of travel.

A servant who uses force in the mistaken but honest belief that he is protecting his master's property does an act incidental to his employment rendering the master liable (*Poland* v. *John Parr & Sons* (C.A., 1927)). Clearly, though, punishment administered during the course of a private altercation which ensues after the need to protect the master's property no longer exists is not within the course of employment (*Warren* v. *Henly's Ltd.* (H.C., 1948)).

The final question to be considered is the extent of a master's liability for the servant who acts dishonestly for his own benefit. In *Morris* v. *C.W. Martin & Sons Ltd.* (C.A., 1966) the defendants' employee stole a coat entrusted to him for cleaning. Whether, as was suggested, the defendants were in breach of their primary duty as bailees, they could equally have been regarded as vicariously liable for their servant's wrongful mode of performing that which he was employed to do, namely to keep the coat safe for its owner. This case has since been approved by the Privy Council. A different problem emerges where the servant abuses his position for fraudulent purposes. In this case, if a master makes it appear to third parties that the servant has authority to do acts of the type in question, he may be estopped from denying that the servant had any authority in fact. It is not enough that the servant's employment provides an opportunity for the commission of the wrong. The essential feature is that it is the position in which the employer places his servant that enables him to perpetrate the fraud whilst acting within the scope of the authority that he appears to have. Thus, in *Lloyd* v. *Grace Smith & Co.* (H.L., 1912) solicitors were held liable for the fraud of their managing clerk in inducing the plaintiff to execute documents which he falsely stated were necessary to effect a sale of her cottages, but which amounted to a conveyance of the property to himself. In fraud cases, therefore, the parameters of the course of employment are set by the scope of authority so that, in *Armagas Ltd.* v. *Mundogas S.A.* (C.A., 1985) the plaintiff's contention that a servant could be acting beyond the scope of his authority but within the course of his employment was rejected. Similarly, if the plaintiff is unaware that the fraudulent servant is the defendant's employee he cannot claim to have relied upon the servant's apparent authority and the defendant will not be liable unless, of course, the servant was within the scope of his actual authority (*Kooragang Investments Pty. Ltd.* v. *Richardson & Wrench Ltd.* (P.C., 1982)).

Joint liability
Where a servant commits a tort in the course of his employment both he and his master are liable as joint tortfeasors. This means that if the master satisfies the judgment he may be able to claim contribution from his servant under the Civil Liability (Contribution) Act 1978. Additionally he may (at least in theory) be able to recover from his servant under the principle in *Lister* v. *Romford Ice and Cold Storage Co. Ltd.* (H.L., 1957) where damages equivalent to an indemnity were awarded to a master, who, having met the plaintiff's claim, sued his negligent employee for breach of an implied term in his employment contract that he would exercise reasonable care. In practice, however, the *Lister* principle is virtually defunct in view of an undertaking by employers' liability insurers that they would not seek to recover from an individual employee except where there was evidence of collusion or wilful misconduct.

INDEPENDENT CONTRACTORS

In general, an employer is not vicariously liable for the negligence of an independent contractor in carrying out his work. He is of course liable if he authorises or ratifies the tort, as he is if he is personally negligent, for example by selecting an incompetent contractor or failing to give proper instructions or supervision. In addition, he may be under a non-delegable duty of care which cannot be discharged merely by entrusting performance to a contractor. It is worth noting that liability in all of these instances is not vicarious but arises as a result of a breach of a primary duty owed by the employer to the plaintiff. The remainder of this section deals with the employer's so-called non-delegable duties.

Common law

1. Withdrawal of support from neighbouring land
Where one of two adjoining landowners is entitled to support from the other and that other, either himself or through his contractor, undermines that support causing damage to his neighbour's land or building, he is liable (*Bower* v. *Peate* (H.C., 1876)).

2. Operations on the highway
Where a contractor is employed to do work on or adjoining the highway which creates a danger to users of the highway, the employer remains liable. So, in *Tarry* v. *Ashton* (H.C., 1876), where a contractor negligently fitted a lamp to the side of a house with the

result that it fell and injured a passer-by, the employer was held liable. Although this principle applies to dangers created in any place along which the public may lawfully pass, no liability attaches to a person using the highway merely for the purposes of lawful passage. Thus, if a motor vehicle is negligently repaired by a contractor, the owner is not liable for an accident caused by the unroadworthy state of the vehicle (*Phillips* v. *Britannia Hygienic Laundry Co. Ltd.* (H.C., 1923)). Nor is there liability in respect of work carried out near the highway. In *Salsbury* v. *Woodland* (C.A., 1970), the employer was held not liable when his contractor negligently cut down a tree in his front garden and, in so doing, fouled some telephone wires which collapsed onto the highway and caused an accident.

3. Master's duty to servant

The non-delegable nature of this common law duty is dealt with in Chapter 7.

4. Extra-hazardous activities

Where the contractor's work, by its very nature, involves a special danger to others, it seems that the employer will be liable for the contractor's default. In *Honeywill and Stein Ltd.* v. *Larkin Bros. Ltd.* (C.A., 1934) the plaintiffs were held liable where the defendants, whom they had employed to take photographs inside a theatre, negligently caused a fire in their use of magnesium flash powder. This principle probably applies only to acts involving the use of things regarded in law as "dangerous in themselves," of which fire and explosives are obvious examples. Since there is nothing inherently dangerous in the operation of felling a tree, *Salsbury* v. *Woodland* (C.A., 1970) was held not to come within this head of liability.

5. Nuisance, Rylands v. Fletcher and fire

The extent of an employer's liability in these instances is dealt with in Chapters 11 and 12.

6. Other cases

There seems to be no general principle which can be extracted from the examples discussed, and the courts may come to recognise new types of case giving rise to a non-delegable duty. A recent illustration is *Rogers* v. *Night Riders* (C.A., 1983) in which the plaintiff was injured when the door of a mini-cab flew open. Although the vehicle was owned and maintained by the driver, an independent contractor, the mini-cab firm was nevertheless held to be in breach of a primary duty owed to the plaintiff.

Statutory duties

Where a statute imposes an obligation upon a person to do a particular thing, he cannot escape liability by delegation to an independent contractor. If the statute empowers a person to do something which would otherwise be unlawful, that person will generally be liable for the negligence of his contractor (*Hardaker* v. *Idle D.C.* (C.A., 1896)). The precise nature of the duty depends, however, upon the construction of the Act.

Casual or collateral negligence

It is the nature of the work, and not merely the performance of it, which may cast upon the employer a non-delegable duty. He is therefore not liable for the casual or collateral negligence of his independent contractor because that does not involve him in any breach of duty. Collateral negligence is negligence purely incidental to the particular act the contractor was employed to do. Thus, in *Padbury* v. *Holliday and Greenwood Ltd.* (C.A., 1912) the defendants were not liable when their sub-contractor, in fixing a casement, negligently left a tool on the window sill which the wind blew onto a passer-by below. By contrast, in *Holliday* v. *National Telephone Co.* (C.A., 1899) the defendants employed a plumber to carry out work on the highway. The plumber negligently dipped his blowlamp into molten solder and the plaintiff was injured in the ensuing explosion. Reversing the decision of the Divisional Court, the Court of Appeal held the employer liable, though the distinction between this and the *Padbury* case is not easy to see.

VEHICLE OWNERS

A vehicle owner who allows another to drive it in his presence makes such a person his agent and is liable for his negligent driving. So too, if a person has authority to drive on behalf of, or for the purposes of, the owner, the latter is vicariously liable for his negligence even though not himself present in the vehicle (*Ormrod* v. *Crosville Motor Services Ltd.* (C.A., 1953)). The leading case of *Launchbury* v. *Morgans* (H.L., 1973) establishes that the owner is not liable simply for permitting another to use the vehicle for his own purposes. It must be shown that the driver was using it for the owner's purposes under delegation of some task or duty, and the mere fact that the owner has an interest in the safety of the vehicle's occupants is not sufficient. Nor, according to *Norwood* v. *Navan* (C.A., 1981), is a wife who uses her husband's car to go on a shopping expedition acting for his purposes under delegation of a task or duty so as to make him vicariously liable.

CHAPTER 15

SAMPLE EXAMINATION QUESTIONS AND ANSWER PLANS

QUESTION 1

Arthur is driving his car along a busy suburban road and discussing with his front seat passenger, George, the cricket match which they have just attended. Both have consumed a considerable amount of alcohol and Arthur, who fails to see a school crossing warden holding up the traffic, strikes and injures Jane, a schoolchild using the crossing. The car then hits a lamp-post and George is thrown through the wind-screen and sustains severe facial injuries. Jane's mother, Mary, was, at the time of the accident, talking to a teacher in the school playground some 50 yards from, and out of sight of, the crossing. She hears the screech of brakes and a child's scream, and, knowing that Jane was using the crossing, collapses with severe shock.

Discuss the liability of Arthur to George, Jane and Mary.

ANSWER PLAN

Arthur may be liable to George, Jane and Mary in the tort of negligence.

1. Arthur's liability to George

(a) As a user of the highway Arthur owes a duty of care to all those whom he can reasonably foresee may suffer injury as a consequence of his acts or omissions [Lord Atkin in *Donoghue* v. *Stevenson*—the neighbour principle]. He therefore owes a duty to George.

(b) Arthur must drive to the standard of the reasonably competent, qualified motorist and, in failing to keep a proper lookout or failing to slow down at a controlled crossing, is clearly in breach of his duty, especially in view of the magnitude of the risk.

(c) The injury to George is caused by Arthur's negligent driving and is reasonably foreseeable. Arthur is therefore liable for George's injuries, subject to any defence.

(d) Arthur will be able to raise the defence of contributory negligence. *Volenti* will not apply, however, because of section 149 of the Road Traffic Act 1988 (see *Pitts* v. *Hunt*). Contributory negligence will almost certainly be a defence for two reasons: first, the facts suggest that George was not wearing a seat-belt (see *Froom* v. *Butcher*), and, secondly, there is authority for the view that a person who takes a lift with a driver, who, to his knowledge, has been drinking and whose ability to drive is thereby impaired, is contributorily negligent (see *Owens* v. *Brimmell*). Provided that George's injuries have been caused or increased by his failure to wear a seat belt, his damages will be reduced on both counts by such an amount as the court thinks just and equitable (Law Reform (Contributory Negligence) Act 1945).

2. Arthur's liability to Jane

Arthur is in breach of the duty which he owes to Jane and is therefore liable in respect of her injuries, for the same reasons that he is liable to George. There are no defences available on the facts.

3. Arthur's liability to Mary

Arthur will be liable to Mary in accordance with the House of Lords decision in *McLoughlin* v. *O'Brian* if shock to Mary was reasonably foreseeable. The shock must manifest itself in some recognisable physical or emotional injury. In determining whether shock is reasonably foreseeable, factors that may be taken into account (though they are not conclusive of the matter) are the degree of relationship between Mary and the victim (very close in this case), the spatial and temporal proximity of Mary to the scene of the accident, and the means by which the shock was caused. Mary is within earshot, though out of sight of, the accident and she may have recognised her child's scream. The shock appears to have been attributable to what Mary perceived through her own unaided senses and she is therefore likely to succeed.

QUESTION 2

Paddy is employed by Jerrybuild Ltd. as a labourer on a building site. Statutory regulations imposed upon construction companies and their employees provide that all persons working on building sites shall wear protective helmets. While climbing a ladder, Paddy, who is not wearing a helmet, is struck on the head by a brick which has been negligently dislodged from an overhead platform by his colleague, Murphy. Paddy falls from the ladder, sustaining severe injuries.

Although Jerrybuild Ltd. has warned its employees of the regulations and does provide helmets at the site, it is common practice for workers not to wear the hats and the site foreman has taken no steps to ensure that the statutory provisions are observed.

Advise Paddy whether he may successfully sue Jerrybuild Ltd.

ANSWER PLAN

Paddy may bring an action against Jerrybuild Ltd. for breach of statutory duty or for breach of their common law duty. Alternatively, he may sue Jerrybuild Ltd. vicariously for the negligence of Murphy.

1. Breach of statutory duty

(a) Paddy must first establish that Parliament intended that a civil action would lie in respect of a breach of the regulations. This is a matter of statutory interpretation, but there is insufficient information in the question. However, industrial safety regulations invariably do confer a right of action.

(b) Assuming that he can sue, he must prove that the duty was owed to him—no difficulty here, the wording of the regulations is clear and unambiguous.

(c) He must prove that the employer is in breach—again, no difficulty because the duty appears to be strict ("shall wear") and it is cast upon J. Ltd. (see, *e.g. John Summers Ltd.* v. *Frost*).

(d) He must show that the damage is of a type which the Act was designed to prevent, so presumably no problem here.

(e) Causation—Paddy must now show that Jerrybuild's breach caused the damage and this calls for a discussion of *Ginty* v. *Belmont Building Supplies Ltd.* If there is some fault on the part of J. Ltd. (evidenced by the fact that employees commonly do not wear the hats and no steps have been taken to enforce the regulations) Paddy can still succeed (see, *e.g. Boyle* v. *Kodak Ltd.*). It is no defence for J. Ltd. to say that they entrusted performance of their duty to the site foreman.

2. Breach of common law duty

(a) The nature of the duty is outlined in *Wilson's and Clyde Coal Co.* v. *English* and is owed to each employee individually.

(b) Is there a breach? Duty is to take reasonable care to provide, *inter alia*, safe plant and equipment. J. Ltd. should warn Paddy about the use of safety helmets (see, *e.g. Bux* v. *Slough Metals Ltd.*).

(c) Causation—is Jerrybuild's breach a cause of the accident or is it Paddy's own fault? The same argument applies as for breach of statutory duty.

3. Vicarious liability of J. Ltd.

Paddy can sue J. Ltd. vicariously for Murphy's negligence, assuming Murphy is a servant acting within the course of his employment (there is no evidence to suggest otherwise).

4. Defences

(a) *Volenti non fit injuria*—not available where Paddy sues J. Ltd. for breach of their statutory or common law duty, but otherwise, in theory, yes (*I.C.I. Ltd.* v. *Shatwell*). Very unlikely in this case—he does not consent to Murphy's negligence either.

(b) Contributory negligence—most likely that his conduct amounts to an unreasonable failure to care for his own safety. Damages will be reduced on a "just and equitable" basis under the 1945 Law Reform (Contributory Negligence) Act.

QUESTION 3

Eva, a spiritualist medium, complains that her next door neighbour, Adam, is having his house demolished and rebuilt by Jerrybuild Limited, a firm of building contractors. The work is being conducted until late at night, disturbing Eva's evening relaxation and preventing her from communicating with spiritual forces, with the result that she has lost clients. She has complained to Adam and to Jerrybuild's foreman about the noise, but since this complaint the workmen on the site have increased the noise whenever they think she is conducting a seance. She has now discovered that vibrations from the demolition activities have caused cracks to appear in the walls of her house, though other houses in the vicinity are unaffected.

Advise Eva.

ANSWER PLAN

Eva may be able to bring an action against Adam and Jerrybuild Ltd. in private nuisance or possibly under the rule in *Rylands* v. *Fletcher* or in negligence for the damage to her house.

1. Nuisance

(a) A private nuisance should be defined. The aim of the law is to achieve a balance between the conflicting interests of neighbouring occupiers. It should be noted that Eva, as an occupier, has a sufficient interest in land to maintain an action.

(b) The essence of a nuisance is that it is continuous or recurrent and, in order to succeed, Eva must show that the interference is unreasonable.

(c) Note that there is both interference with enjoyment and tangible physical damage. What factors, then, are relevant in determining whether the interference is unreasonable and therefore unlawful? The duration and extent of the interference (the work is being conducted until late at night) must be considered, as well as the nature of the defendant's conduct. Is Eva's use of her land abnormally sensitive? (see, *e.g. Bridlington Relay* v. *Y.E.B.*; *Robinson* v. *Kilvert*). But note that once a nuisance is established she can recover even in respect of delicate operations (*McKinnon Industries* v. *Walker*), though consider the nature of her loss. As far as the damage to her house is concerned see, too, *Hoare & Co.* v. *McAlpine*. There is evidence of spite on the part of J. Ltd., so explain what effect that may have (see, *e.g. Christie* v. *Davey*; *Hollywood Silver Fox Farm* v. *Emmett*).

(d) Who can Eva sue? J. Ltd. are liable as the creators of the nuisance, but Adam, too, may be liable as occupier, on the basis that he has invited them onto his land and the work involved creates a foreseeable risk of nuisance (see, *e.g. Matania* v. *National Provincial Bank Ltd.*). There is authority to suggest that an occupier will generally be liable for the defaults of his contractor (*Spicer* v. *Smee*). What effect, if any, does the spite of J. Ltd. have on Adam's liability?

(e) If Eva can establish a prima facie case, are there any defences? There would appear to be none, except that the use of her land may be abnormally sensitive (see above), though this would appear to be very unlikely on the facts.

(f) Eva may claim damages and an injunction to control the times at which the work is carried out (see, *e.g. Kennaway* v. *Thompson*) or to prevent the work altogether if it cannot be done without damaging the structure of her house.

2. Rylands v. Fletcher

After stating the rule in *Rylands* v. *Fletcher*, attention should be directed towards whether the activities in question amount to a non-natural use of land. According to *Mason* v. *Levy Autoparts of*

England Ltd. regard may be had to the manner in which the work is conducted to see whether Adam and J. Ltd. have created an abnormal risk (see, too *Rickards* v. *Lothian*). Although the "escape" of the vibrations has caused damage to her property she may not succeed if her house is unusually susceptible to that damage (but *cf. Hoare & Co.* v. *McAlpine*). Adam is liable for the default of his contractors.

3. Negligence
There may be liability in negligence if it can be proved that the activities of J. Ltd. were conducted in such a manner as to create an unreasonable and foreseeable risk of damage to Eva's property.

QUESTION 4

Jake owns and occupies a large house in the country and has recently been the victim of a number of burglary attempts. In order to deter burglars he allows his Alsatian dog, which, because of its excitable temperament, is secured to a kennel during the day-time, to roam free in the garden at night. One evening Hank, intending to burgle the premises, gains access to the garden and is attacked and bitten by the dog. Hearing Hank's shouts, police constable Merryweather, who has been asked by Jake to keep a careful watch on the house, forces the bolt on a side gate and rushes into the garden. Knowing of the dog's excitable nature Merryweather attempts to placate the animal and is himself bitten. The dog runs through the open gate, crosses the road and jumps through a fence into a field owned by Jake's neighbour Giles, where it attacks and kills a sheep. When Giles discovers the sheep early next morning he lies in wait for the dog and shoots and kills it as he sees it near his chicken run.

Advise Jake as to his liability and whether he may successfully sue for the loss of his dog.

ANSWER PLAN

1. Jake's liability to Hank
(a) Jake may be liable to Hank in accordance with section 2 of the Animals Act 1971. Does the Alsatian belong to a dangerous species (see *Cummings* v. *Granger*)? If not, consider section 2(2) of the Act to see if the three conditions are satisfied. The first condition would appear to be in that, even if the damage is not of a kind which the animal was likely to cause, it was of a kind that was likely to be severe. The second is satisfied if the likelihood of its being severe is

due to abnormal characteristics or normal in the particular circumstances (see *Cummings* v. *Granger*). Those characteristics must be known to Jake; actual knowledge is required and that may be inferred from the fact that it is secured during the day because of its excitable temperament. Jake is prima facie strictly liable subject to any defences, because he is the keeper of the dog (explain who the "keeper" is).

(b) Defences under the Act include contributory negligence, voluntary assumption of the risk and that the damage was wholly due to Hank's fault. Do any of these apply (see *Cummings* v. *Granger*)? The special defence in section 5(3) of the Act applies if the keeping of the Alsatian as a guard dog is reasonable (*Note*—the Guard Dogs Act 1975 does not apply to land around a private dwelling).

2. Jake's liability to Merryweather

The same considerations apply to Merryweather as to Hank, and Jake is prima facie liable in accordance with section 2(2) of the Act. Could it be argued that Merryweather voluntarily assumes the risk of injury? This is most unlikely in the circumstances, nor would there be much force in the argument that the damage was wholly due to his fault (though this is not completely beyond question). He did, however, try to placate the animal, of whose vicious characteristics he was aware, and, depending on the circumstances (*e.g.* was the dog actually attacking Hank at the time?) he could be contributorily negligent and may have his damages reduced.

3. Jake's liability to Giles

There is strict liability under section 3 of the Animals Act in respect of the killing or injuring of livestock by a dog. The sheep is within the definition of "livestock" (see section 11 of the Act) and liability is imposed upon the keeper of the dog (see section 6(3)). Jake is therefore liable to Giles for the loss of the sheep and there would appear to be no defence (*Note*—In particular, there is no mention in the Act of a defence of act of a stranger, so that the fact that the gate is left open by Merryweather will not avail Jake).

4. Giles' liability to Jake

Giles may have a defence to an action in trespass for killing Jake's dog, in accordance with section 9 of the Animals Act. Giles must prove that he acted for the protection of livestock and was entitled so to act, and that he notified the police within 48 hours. Giles is entitled to act for the protection of the livestock because it is upon his land. Whether he is in fact acting for the protection of either his sheep or his chickens (which fall within the definition of "livestock") depends upon whether the terms of section 9(3) of the Act are satisfied (though, by section 9(4), reasonable belief on Giles' part is sufficient). If, for some reason, the statutory defence is not available, can Giles fall back on the common law (see *Creswell* v. *Sirl*)?

QUESTION 5

In response to a request for a reference, Derek, Fred's present employer, wrote to Fred's prospective employer, John, and informed him that Fred was having an affair with a married woman, Glenda, who worked in the same office. In fact, Fred had once slept with her after an office party two years previously but had since hardly spoken to her. Derek's secretary, Beth, to whom the letter was dictated and who was aware of the precise nature of the relationship between Fred and Glenda, made an extra copy of the letter. Beth showed it to Fred's mother, Mary, her close friend. Derek inadvertently left his copy of the letter lying openly on the desk in his private office where it was seen by Henry, his immediate superior. Henry saw the letter as he was looking for something else on Derek's desk, in Derek's absence.

Discuss the liability of Derek and Beth in defamation to Fred and Glenda.

ANSWER PLAN

1. Derek's liability to Fred

(a) Fred must first prove that the statement is defamatory, so a definition of a defamatory statement is required. It is for the judge to decide whether the statement is capable of being defamatory in law, and for the jury to decide if it is in fact. Derek's statement is prima facie defamatory.

(b) Libel or slander? The letter to John is a libel, and the dictation to Beth a slander (is it actionable *per se* under section 2 of the Defamation Act 1952?)

(c) Fred must prove that the statement refers to him (presumably it does) and that it has been published. There is publication to Beth, John and to Henry. Derek will be liable for publishing to Henry if he carelessly leaves correspondence around where it is foreseeable that others may see it (which may be the case here). Fred may therefore sue Derek subject to any defences.

(d) Defences. Can Derek plead justification or truth? The statement must be substantially true (which seems unlikely), though it is for the jury to decide whether a minor inaccuracy defeats the defence. Qualified privilege is more likely on the basis that Derek has a duty to communicate and John a corresponding interest in receiving the statement. This would ordinarily cover a job reference, but is there a duty to communicate information of this type which probably does not reflect upon Fred's fitness for the post in question? As far as the publication to Beth is concerned, Derek may have a defence if it is reasonable (is it?) and in the ordinary course of business (see *Bryanston Finance* v. *De Vries*). Is qualified privilege a defence with regard to the publication to Henry?

2. Derek's liability to Glenda

(a) Glenda must prove that the statement is defamatory, that it refers to her and that it has been published. The slander to Beth is actionable *per se* (Slander of Women Act 1891).

(b) Defences. The same as in relation to Fred except that qualified privilege is likely to fail on the ground that Derek will have great difficulty in proving that he had a duty to publish to John (assuming that he names or otherwise identifies her, else there is no reference to her).

3. Beth's liability to Fred

Beth publishes a libel to Mary, so she is prima facie liable. The only possible defences are justification (though she must prove the truth of the statement, not merely that another made it) and qualified privilege. Mary may have an interest in receiving the statement but does Beth have a duty to communicate (see *Watt* v. *Longsdon*)? Since she knows the precise nature of the relationship, is there evidence of malice? If so, the privilege (if it existed) is destroyed.

4. Beth's liability to Glenda

The same as with Fred, but could she possibly have a duty to publish to Mary?

INDEX

Notes

Notes

Notes

Notes

Notes